POEMS TO ENJOY: BOOK FOUR

Chosen and Edited by Verner Bickley

5th edition

Proverse Hong Kong

VERNER BICKLEY, MBE, PhD, is a well-known "voice", educationist, and adjudicator, who has held director-level positions in Universities and Government Departments. He is Chairman Emeritus of the English-Speaking Union (HK) and Co-Founder of the International Proverse Prizes for unpublished writing. He travels frequently to judge public-speaking competitions and regularly adjudicates verse and prose speaking and reading, as well as drama and choral speaking.

Dr Bickley's series of graded poetry anthologies – **POEMS TO ENJOY** – is a well-established tool for learning and teaching English at all levels. Useful notes and a teaching guide are included.

Taken as a whole, this five-book series is suitable for all students, teachers and parents. **Book 1** can be used and enjoyed by Primary 1-3 students and **Book 2** by Primary 4-6 students. **Book 3** can be used and enjoyed by Secondary 1-2 students, **Book 4** by Secondary 3-4 students and **Book 5** by secondary 5-6 students. Students, parents and teachers will enjoy and find useful Dr Bickley's selection of poems.

It is strongly recommended that readers also purchase the Third Edition, which is accompanied by a CD containing lively readings of all poems in the book. These recordings assist pronunciation and help those preparing for solo verse speaking and reading, duo and group-work and choral-speaking in Speech Festivals. They also enhance reading experience.

Parents will welcome this book, in all editions, which gives them the opportunity to read aloud with their children.

THIS BOOK IS A PERENNIAL FAVOURITE.

POEMS TO ENJOY

BOOK FOUR

AN ANTHOLOGY OF POEMS

FOR INTERMEDIATE and ADVANCED
STUDENTS AND READERS

WITH TEACHING AND LEARNING NOTES AND GUIDE

**CHOSEN AND EDITED BY
DR VERNER BICKLEY,**
MBE, PhD (Lond.), MA, BA (Hons), DipEd, LRAM,
LGSM, FCIL, FRSA

Proverse Hong Kong

Poems to Enjoy, Book Four.
Chosen and Edited by Verner Bickley.
With teaching and performance notes by Verner Bickley.
5th edition published in Hong Kong by Proverse Hong Kong, February 2019.
Copyright © Verner Bickley, February 2019.
ISBN: 978-988-8491-60-5

Distribution and other enquiries: Proverse Hong Kong, P. O. Box 259, Tung Chung Post Office, Tung Chung, Lantau Island, NT, Hong Kong SAR, China.
E-mail: proverse@netvigator.com Web site: www.proversepublishing.com

Illustrations copyright © Proverse Hong Kong.
Cover design, Proverse Hong Kong and Artist Hong Kong Company.

The right of Verner Bickley to be identified as the anthologiser and editor of this work has been asserted by him in accordance with the Copyright, Designs and Patents Act 1988.

All rights reserved. No part of this publication may be reproduced, stored in a retrieval system, or transmitted, in any form or by any means, electronic, mechanical, photocopying, recording or otherwise, without the prior written permission of the publisher or publisher and author. The book is sold subject to the condition that it shall not, by way of trade or otherwise, be lent, re-sold, hired out or otherwise circulated in any form of binding or cover other than that in which it is published without the publisher's prior written consent and without a similar condition including this condition being imposed on the subsequent owner or purchaser. Please contact Proverse Hong Kong in writing, to request any and all permissions (including but not restricted to republishing, inclusion in anthologies, translation, reading, performance and use as set pieces in examinations and festivals).

Poems to Enjoy, Book Four was first published in the United Kingdom in 1960, by University of London Press Ltd (GB SBN 340 07584 8) copyright © Verner Bickley 1960, with Teaching Notes in a separate volume, copyright © Verner Bickley 1960.
The 3rd edition, published by Proverse Hong Kong in November 2014, is a complete, updated version of the 1st edition, combining Poems and Teaching Notes in one book. Additionally, it includes an audio recording of all the poems in the book.
A 2nd edition was published in 1989 as *Poems to Enjoy Book 4*, part of a three-book series, with audio cassettes, and contains about half of the poems in *Poems to Enjoy, Book Four*, 3rd and 5th editions.

Proverse Hong Kong

British Library Cataloguing in Publication Data (for 3rd edition, with CD)

Poems to enjoy.
Book 4. -- 3rd ed.
1. English poetry. 2. Oral interpretation of poetry--
Juvenile literature. 3. English poetry--Study and teaching
(Secondary) 4. English language--Study and teaching--
Foreign speakers.
I. Bickley, Verner Courtenay.
821'.008-dc23

ISBN-13: 9789888167500

ACKNOWLEDGEMENTS

For permission to use copyright material thanks are due to: Messrs. Dodd Mead & Company for 'Elephant Song' from *Memory Room* and 'Foreboding' from *Vagabond's House* both by Don Blanding (copyright 1928 and 1935); The Clarendon Press for 'The Maker of Cradles' and 'When Beggars Ride' both by Thora Stowell from *100 Poems for Boys and Girls*, The Society of Authors and Dr. John Masefield, O.M., for 'A Wanderer's Song' and 'Cargoes'; John Lane the Bodley Head Ltd. for 'Piper Play' by John Davidson from *Selected Poems* and 'The Destined Hour' by F. L. Lucas from *Many Lands and Times;* The Literary Trustees of Walter de la Mare and Messrs. Faber & Faber Ltd. for 'The Ride-by-Nights' and 'The Old Stone House'; Messrs. Constable & Co. Ltd. for 'Lo Yang' by Arthur Waley; Mrs George Bambridge and Messrs. Macmillan & Co. Ltd. for 'Night Song in the Jungle' by Rudyard Kipling from *Jungle Book;* the Trustees of Rabindranath Tagore and Messrs. Macmillan & Co. Ltd. for 'The Gardener'; Messrs. J. M. Dent & Sons Ltd. for 'The Poultries' by Ogden Nash; the Author's Executor for 'A Piper' by Seumas O'Sullivan; Messrs. Methuen & Co. Ltd. for 'The Island' by A. A. Milne from *When We Were Very Toung;* The Author's Representatives and Messrs. Sidgwick & Jackson Ltd. for 'Romance' and 'India' both by W. J. Turner from *The Hunter and Other Poems,* 'The Bridge' by J. Redwood Anderson from *Walls and Hedges* and 'Vigil' from *The Collected Poems of John Drinkwater;* Messrs. Routledge & Kegan Paul Ltd. for 'The Malay Kris' by Sir Richard Windstedt from *The Malays;* Messrs. A. D. Peters for 'In The Jungle' by Martin Armstrong; The Hogarth Press Ltd. for 'Parachute' by Stanley Snaith; Mr Donald Moore for 'The Towkay' by Margaret Leong from *Air above the Tamarinds;* Messrs. Macmillan & Co. Ltd. for 'When The Plane Dived' by Wilfrid Gibson from *The Alert;* and Messrs. Houghton Mifflin Company, U.S.A. for 'Night With a Wolf' by Bayard Taylor.

In certain cases it has not been possible to trace the copyright holders, but full acknowledgment of any rights not mentioned here will be made in subsequent editions if notification is received.

TO THE READER

This book contains a selection of poems for you to read and enjoy. Poetry is an interesting and special way of expressing human thoughts and feelings. Some poems in this selection tell a story, some express a mood and some describe a scene. To be fully enjoyed, a good many of these poems must be read aloud or heard.

In **Part One** of this book you will find a number of poems which are especially suitable for speaking, either by individuals, or by groups. Whatever the treatment, however, the main purpose is enjoyment and this same purpose applies equally to Parts Two and Three.

Each of the poems in **Part Two** paints a picture in words and describes persons, animals and scenes, many of which you will find familiar. You will find it interesting and profitable to sketch or paint the pictures you see in your mind's eye after you have listened to the poems being read aloud.

All the poems in **Part Three** are narrative poems, poems which tell a story. After you have read these poems yourself or perhaps after hearing a reading of them, you will find a discussion useful to clear up any difficulties.

I hope that the experience of poetry that you gain from reading this selection will encourage you to read more and more poems and perhaps to attempt to write poetry yourself. These activities will help you to improve your English language reading and listening, and also speaking and writing skills. They are also interesting and enjoyable.

We hope you will come to love poetry as much as we do ourselves!

TO ALL PARENTS

It is pleasant to share interests and time with our children and other young people. Poetry is often regarded as difficult. – In reality, some is difficult and some is not difficult. –The poems in this *Poems to Enjoy* series of five books are carefully graded, with adequate notes, to make reading pleasant and understanding accesible at levels suitable for each reader. Whether or not parents are already in the habit of reading poetry in English, they can enjoy reading the poems in this series with their children of all ages and other young people.

TO ALL TEACHERS

This book contains a variety of poems of different degrees of difficulty to suit different ways of learning. The poems in Part One are suitable for reading aloud; those in Part Two are largely descriptive; and each poem in Part Three tells a story. The sequence in which the poems are used is, however, at the teacher's discretion.

The poems can be used as supplementary reading material, for oral work, including practice of stress and rhythm, and for different kinds of listening activities. The descriptive poems should develop and challenge the students' imagination and the 'story' or 'narrative' poems are included because all students like to hear or read a good story, provided that they can understand it. In addition to being enjoyed for themselves, the narrative poems provide material for choral work, for dramatization, discussions and questioning.

All the poems in this collection are suitable for extra-curricular work, for example, verse-speaking, choral-speaking, drama, and words and movement.

Poetry can be integrated successfully with the presentation and practice / activities stage of an English lesson, and if emphasis is placed on enjoyment and if also the students are encouraged to participate fully in the lesson, it can make learning more effective. Poetry develops and broadens the imagination through role-playing, provides training in visual perception, helps in the formation of ideas, and adds a new dimension to group work.

Poetry often explores the possibilities of language and this can help the student to construct a new and different framework from that of his own language, acquire different sequences and make forward guesses.

Poems to Speak

This section contains poems which have a pronounced rhythmic and musical quality. This makes it particularly enjoyable to read them aloud, whether individually, or in chorus, or groups. Because it requires good breath-control, clear enunciation of consonants and precise shaping of vowels, choral speech is valuable as a way of training both ear and voice for all types of solo speech. Whether a poem should be spoken by the class as a whole, by soloists, or by different groups of various sizes, depends upon the teacher's own preferences, and, even better, upon the ideas of the students themselves. When groups are required, it is a good idea to keep them constant for choral work in different lessons. In this way, it is possible to distribute the ablest speakers in the class among the various groups.

Some suggestions for choral arrangements are given in the Teaching/Learning Guide at the end of the book. Each poem which is at all suitable for choral work is, of course, open to much variation, and the suggestions in the Guide should not therefore be taken as obligatory.

Pictures in Poetry
The poems in this section are intended to enhance the students' ability to visualise, in one form or another, what has been described. If the classroom environment is suitable, two or three poems can sometimes be read to create the right atmosphere for a lesson in which the aim is to encourage the students to sketch from the imagination. Once this atmosphere is achieved, the work can begin. When it is complete, the final results can be collected from individuals and shown to the rest of the group or class. Eventually, the students can be encouraged to make their own anthologies by writing out some of the poems from this collection and illustrating them from their own creative work. Pictures and photographs that are similar to scenes in the poems can be brought to the class to be used as the basis for discussion.

The Poet as Storyteller
The poems in this section can be used as material upon which the students can comment and which they can use as the basis for writing their own stories in prose or verse on related themes. The success of the poetry-writing lesson will depend primarily upon the classroom atmosphere; and interruptions from outside the room should, therefore, be avoided as much as is possible. In the concluding stages of each lesson, the students can read their own poems aloud and be invited to make suggestions and comments.

The Teaching and Learning Notes and Guide
The Teaching and Learning Notes and Guide contain suggestions for choral arrangements; definitions and explanations of words and phrases; suggestions for illustrative work and story-writing and questions for discussion.

Timeless and traditional

The books contain traditional and timeless poems, as well as poems that inform us how children and adults thought at different periods of time, including at an earlier period of technological sophistication. Different scenes, countries and historical periods are evoked, as well as different personalities and relationships.

Moral Education

The poems express many emotions – tenderness, joy, amusement, wonder, defiance – and elicit many others – sympathy, concern, helpfulness, admiration for self-sacrifice and loyalty. Some are humourous ('The Milton Abbas Rhyme', 'Elegy on the Death of a Mad Dog', 'The Gentleman on the Gate', 'The Common Cormorant').

There are cautionary tales ('Pelters of Pyramids', which teaches respect for ancient cultures; 'The Story of Johnny Head-In-Air', which teaches practicality; 'The Shepherd Boy and the Wolf', which teaches us not to "cry 'wolf'"). 'The Frog and The Crow' is a lesson in analysing a situation and identifying a confidence trickster. 'The Three Fishers' is a lesson in stoicism in the face of the dangers and sadnesses of life.

Some encourage cheerfulness and the ability to enjoy recreative activity amidst a life of manual labour ('Piper Play!', 'A Piper'). Some show how a person in a high position can gain respect by showing consideration for another being ('The Emperor and the Bird's Nest'). Some of the descriptive poems express and teach observation and appreciation of the natural world ("from 'The Gardener'", 'Amphibian'). Some pay tribute to the power of the imagination ('Romance').

A range of values is implicit in many. For example, 'The Maker of Cradles' asks us to value the artisan's creativity and skill and the objects he produces, as well as the value of human love. The same poem also implies that the love of a mother is equally valuable, irrespective of whether she can or cannot afford to purchase expensive or beautiful material gifts for her child.

The audio recording (3rd edition only)
In the audio recording two adult English native-speakers, who enjoy reading aloud, speak the poems. On another occasion, of course, they each might read the poems differently. There is no need to copy or ask students to copy their readings. However, these recordings will be useful in several ways. They will serve to make the meaning of the poems clearer. They offer interpretations of the poems and examples of the use of stress, pause, variety of pitch, enjambement, tone, and similar. They give good guidance as to the pronunciation of words that may be less familiar to readers. They are enjoyable in themselves. Among the total number, some are bravura performances; particularly noteworthy are Verner Bickley's reading of 'The Bridge', 'The Hangman's Tree' and 'The Highwayman' and Gillian Bickley's reading of 'The Kite' and 'The Three Fishers'.

Variety may usefully be introduced in the use of the text and the recording. Sometimes, the text could be read first, sometimes the recording could be listened to first. Sometimes both could be used at the same time.

Write to us!
Teachers, students and parents are encouraged to write to us to share their experiences. We would be very interested to know which approach was most useful to you and with what particular poems was this true. The Proverse website, proversepublishing.com makes provision for you to contact us with your comments.

Contents

Acknowledgements   5
To The Reader   6
To All Students, Parents and Teachers   7

PART ONE: POEMS TO SPEAK

TITLE	AUTHOR
The Wraggle Taggle Gypsies	Traditional
There Was a Frog	Old Ballad
The Milton Abbas Rhyme	Anon.
The Train	C. H. Crandall
A Dutch Picture	H. W. Longfellow
A Long Time Ago	Anon.
Foreboding	Don Blanding
Elephant Song	Don Blanding
Song of the Fox	Traditional
The Hunt is Up	Sixteenth Century Song
A Carrion Crow	Folk Song
The Maker of Cradles	Thora Stowell
Bound to California	Sea Shanty
A Wanderer's Song	John Masefield
Merry are the Bells	Anon.
A Fox Jumped Up	Old Rhyme
Piper Play!	John Davidson
The Crocodile	Folk Song
Sic Vita	William Strode
Sic Vita	William Browne
When Beggars Ride	Thora Stowell
The Frog and the Crow	Anon.
Casey Jones	Old American Ballad
A Naughty Boy	John Keats
Ye Spotted Snakes	William Shakespeare
The One-Eyed Riley	Anon.
Battle Song	John Fletcher
The Shepherd Boy and the Wolf	From Æsop
The Gentleman on the Gate	Lewis Carroll

PART TWO: PICTURES IN POETRY

TITLE	AUTHOR
The Ride-By-Nights	Walter de la Mare
Night Song in the Jungle	Rudyard Kipling
From The Gardener	Rabindranath Tagore
Lo-Yang	Arthur Waley
Three Young Rats	Anon.
Amphibian	Robert Browning
If	Anon.
From Evening	Mary Coleridge
The Common Cormorant	Anon.
The Snail	William Cowper
Snake	Emily Dickinson
The Shell	Alfred, Lord Tennyson
The Poultries	Ogden Nash
The Wind in the Grass	Ralph W. Emerson
Vigil	John Drinkwater
A Piper	Seamus O'Sullivan
The Island	A. A. Milne
The Housekeeper	Charles Lamb
Romance	W. J. Turner
The Lion's Skeleton	Charles Tennyson-Turner
The Bridge	J. Redwood Anderson
The Old Stone House	Walter de la Mare
I Like to See…	Emily Dickinson
The Cane-Bottom'd Chair	William Makepeace Thackeray
In the Jungle	Martin Armstrong
The Malay Kris	Sir Richard Winstedt
Parachute	Stanley Snaith
India	W. J. Turner
Cargoes	John Masefield
Deserted	Madison Cawein
With Ships the Sea was Sprinkled	William Wordsworth

PART THREE: THE POET AS STORYTELLER

TITLE	AUTHOR
The Hangman's Tree	Anon.
The Slave's Dream	H. W. Longfellow
The Towkay	Margaret Leong
Ballad	John Sterling
An Incident of the French Camp	Robert Browning
The Glove and the Lions	Leigh Hunt
The Knight's Leap	Charles Kingsley
Paul Revere's Ride	H. W. Longfellow
Annabel Lee	EdgarAllen Poe
The Emperor and the Bird's Nest	H. W. Longfellow
When the Plane Dived	Wilfrid Gibson
The Kite	John Freeman
The Sailor's Consolation	Charles Dibdin
The Beggar Maid	Alfred, Lord Tennyson
The Three Fishers	Charles Kingsley
The Goose	Alfred, Lord Tennyson
The Old Navy	Captain Marryat
Pelters of Pyramids	Richard Hengist Horne
The Destined Hour	F. L. Lucas
The Vision of Belshazzar	Lord Byron
The Colubriad	William Cowper
Night with a Wolf	J. B. Taylor
Elegy on the Death of a Mad Dog	Oliver Goldsmith
The Rebel Soldier	J. B. Taylor
Shameful Death	Oliver Goldsmith
From 'Horatius'	Lord Macaulay
The Marriage Ring	George Crabbe
Abou Ben Adhem	Leigh Hunt
The Charge of the Light Brigade	Alfred, Lord Tennyson

Introduction to Teaching and Learning Notes and Guide   139
Teaching and Learning Notes and Guide   142
About the Editor   189
About Proverse Hong Kong / The Proverse Prizes   191

Part One

Poems to Speak

THE WRAGGLE TAGGLE GYPSIES

Three gypsies stood at the castle gate,
    They sang so high, they sang so low,
The lady sate in her chamber late,
    Her heart it melted away as snow.

They sang so sweet, they sang so shrill,
    That fast her tears began to flow.
And she laid down her silken gown,
    Her golden rings and all her show.

She plucked off her high-heeled shoes,
    A-made of Spanish leather, O!
She would in the street, with her bare, bare feet,
    All out in the wind and weather, O!

It was late last night, when my lord came home,
    Enquiring for his lady, O!
The servants said on every hand,
    "She's gone with the wraggle taggle gypsies, O!"

"O saddle me to my milk-white steed,
    Go and fetch me my pony, O!
That I may ride and seek my bride,
    Who is gone with the wraggle taggle gypsies, O!"

O he rode high and he rode low,
    He rode through the woods and copses too.
Until he came to an open field,
    And there he espied his a-lady, O!

"What makes you leave your house and land?
  What makes you leave your money, O?
What makes you leave your new-wedded lord,
To go with the wraggle taggle gypsies, O?"

"What care I for my house and my land?
  What care I for my money, O?
What care I for my new wedded lord?
  I'm off with the wraggle taggle gypsies, O!"

"Last night you slept on a goose-feather bed,
  With the sheet turned down so bravely, O!
And to-night you'll sleep in a cold open field,
  Along with the wraggle taggle gypsies, O!"

"What care I for a goose-feather bed,
With the sheet turned down so bravely, O?
For to-night I shall sleep in a cold, open field,
Along with the wraggle taggle gypsies, O!"

Traditional

THERE WAS A FROG

There was a frog lived in a well,
Whipsee diddle-dee dandy dee;
There was a frog lived in a well,
And a merry mouse in a mill,
With a harum scarum, diddle dum darum,
Whipsee diddle-dee dandy dee.

This frog he would a-wooing ride,
Whipsee diddle-dee dandy dee;
This frog he would a-wooing ride,
And on a snail he got astride,
With a harum scarum, diddle dum darum,
Whipsee diddle-dee dandy dee.

He rode till he came to my Lady Mouse Hall,
Whipsee diddle-dee dandy dee;
He rode till he came to my Lady Mouse Hall,
And there he did both knock and call,
With a harum scarum, diddle dum darum,
Whipsee diddle-dee, dandy dee.

"Miss Mouse, Miss Mouse, I'm come to thee,"
Whipsee, diddle-dee, dandy dee;
"Miss Mouse, Miss Mouse, I'm come to thee,
To see if thou canst fancy me."
With a harum scarum, diddle dum darum,
Whipsee diddle-dee, dandy dee.

"Oh answer will I give you none,"
Whipsee diddle-dee dandy dee;
"Oh answer will I give you none
Until my Uncle Rat comes home,"

With a harum scarum, diddle dum darum,
Whipsee diddle-dee dandy dee.

And when her Uncle Rat came home,
Whipsee diddle-dee dandy dee;
And when her Uncle Rat came home,
"Who's been here since I've been gone?"
With a harum, scarum, diddle dum darum,
Whipsee diddle-dee dandy dee.

"There's been a worthy gentleman,"
Whipsee, diddle-dee dandy dee;
"There's been a worthy gentleman,
That's been here since you've been gone."
With a harum, scarum, diddle dum darum,
Whipsee, diddle-dee, dandy dee.
The frog he came whistling through the brook,
Whipsee diddle-dee dandy dee;
The frog he came whistling through the brook,
And there he met with a dainty duck.
With a harum, scarum, diddle dum darum,
Whipsee, diddle-dee, dandy dee.

The duck she swallowed him up with a quack,
Whipsee diddle-dee dandy dee;
The duck she swallowed him up with a quack,
So there's an end of my history book.
With a harum, scarum, diddle dum darum,
Whipsee, diddle-dee dandy dee.

Old Ballad

THE MILTON ABBAS RHYME

St Catherine, St Catherine,
O lend me your aid,
And grant that I never
May die an old maid!

A husband, St Catherine!
A good one, St Catherine!
But any one better
Than no one, St Catherine!
A husband, St Catherine!

Handsome, St Catherine!
Rich, St Catherine!
Young, St Catherine!
Soon, St Catherine!

Anon.

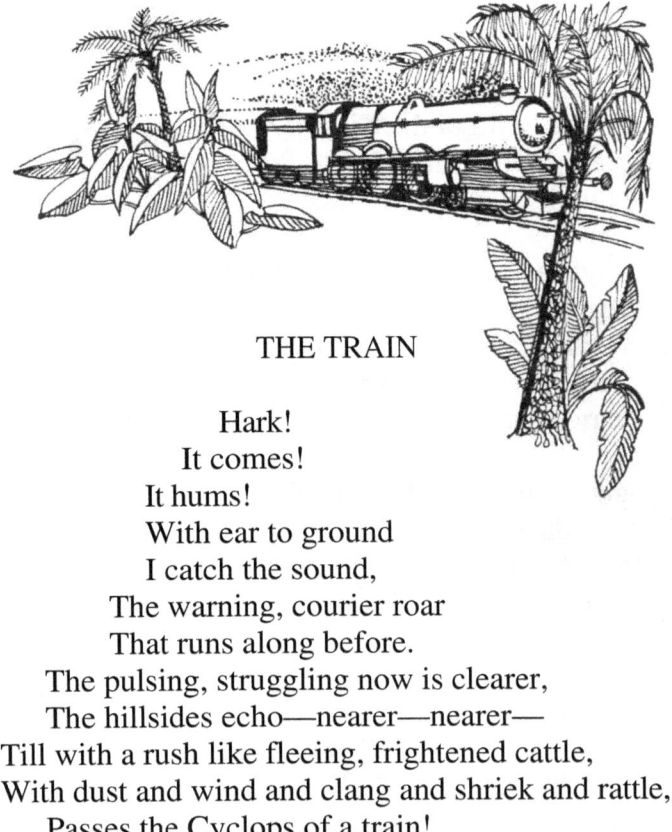

THE TRAIN

Hark!
It comes!
It hums!
With ear to ground
I catch the sound,
The warning, courier roar
That runs along before.
The pulsing, struggling now is clearer,
The hillsides echo—nearer—nearer—
Till with a rush like fleeing, frightened cattle,
With dust and wind and clang and shriek and rattle,
Passes the Cyclops of a train!
And there's a fair face at a pane.
Like a piano string
The rails, unburdened, sing;
The white smoke flies
Up to the skies;
The sound
Is drowned.
Hark!

C. H. Crandall

A DUTCH PICTURE

Simon Danz has come home again,
    From cruising about with his buccaneers;
He has singed the beard of the King of Spain,
And carried away the Dean of Jaén
    And sold him in Algiers.

In his house by the Maese, with its roof of tiles,
    And weathercocks flying aloft in air,
There are silver tankards of antique styles,
Plunder of convent and castle, and piles
    Of carpets rich and rare.

In his tulip-garden there by the town,
    Overlooking the sluggish stream,
With his Moorish cap and dressing-gown,
The old sea-captain, hale and brown,
    Walks in a waking dream.

A smile in his grey mustachio lurks
    Whenever he thinks of the King of Spain,
And the listed tulips look like Turks,
And the silent gardener as he works
    Is changed to the Dean of Jaén.

The windmills on the outermost
    Verge of the landscape in the haze,
To him are towers on the Spanish coast,
With whiskered sentinels at their post,
    Though this is the river Maese.

But when the winter rains begin,
    He sits and smokes by the blazing brands,
And old sea-faring men come in,
Goat-bearded, grey, and with double chin,
    And rings upon their hands.

They sit there in the shadow and shine
    Of the flickering fire of the winter night;
Figures in colour and design
Like those by Rembrandt of the Rhine
    Half darkness and half light.

And they talk of ventures lost or won,
    And their talk is ever and ever the same,
While they drink the red wine of Tarragon,
From the cellars of some Spanish Don,
    Or convent set on flame.

So he thinks he shall take to the sea again
    For one more cruise with his buccaneers,
To singe the beard of the King of Spain,
And capture another Dean of Jaén
    And sell him in Algiers.

W. H. Longfellow

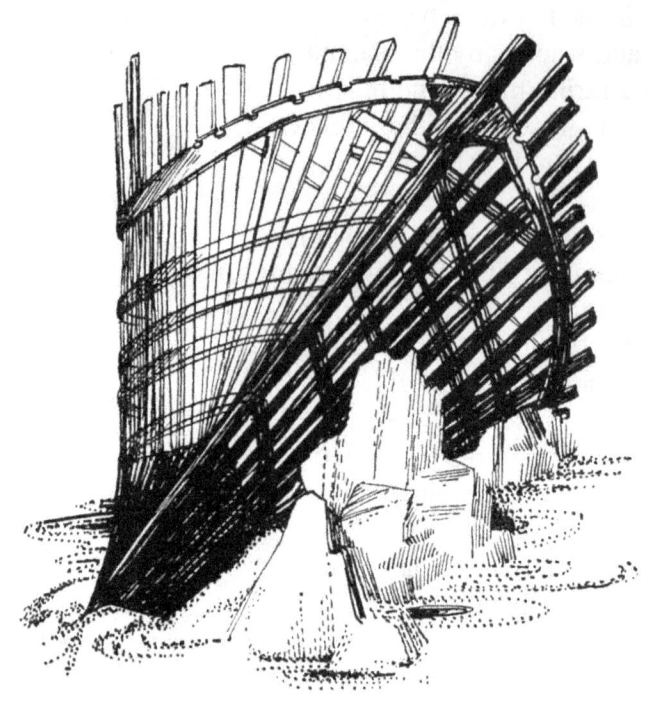

A LONG TIME AGO

A long, long, time, and a long time ago,
   To me way hay, ohio;
A long, long, time and a long time ago,
   A long time ago.

A smart Yankee packet lay out in the bay,
   To me way hay, ohio;
A-waiting for a fair wind to get under way,
   A long time ago.

With all her poor sailors all sick and all sore,
    To me way hay, ohio;
For they'd drunk all their lime-juice, and could get no more,
    A long time ago.

With all her poor sailors all sick and all sad,
    To me way hay, ohio;
For they'd drunk all their lime-juice, and no more could be had,
    A long time ago.

She was waiting for a fair wind to get under way,
    To me way hay, ohio;
She was waiting for a fair wind to get under way,
    A long time ago.

If she hasn't had a fair wind she's lying there still,
    To me way hay, ohio;
If she hasn't had a fair wind she's lying there still,
    A long time ago.

Anon.

FOREBODING

Zoom, zoom, zoom!
That is the sound of the surf,
As the great green waves rush up the shore
With murderous, thundering, ominous roar;
And leave drowned dead things by my door.
Zoom, zoom, zoom!
Sh-wsh-wsh! Sh-wsh-wsh! Sh-wsh-wsh!
That is the sound of the tow
As it slips and slithers along the sand
Like terrible, groping, formless hands,
That drag at my beach house where it stands.
Sh-wsh-wsh! Sh-wsh-wsh! Sh-wsh-wsh!
Ee-oh-i-oo! Ee-oh-i-oo! Ee-oh-i-oo!
That is the sound of the wind.
It wails like a banshee adrift in space.
It threatens to scatter my driftwood place.
It slashes the sand like spite in my face.
Ee-oh-i-oo! Ee-oh-i-oo! Ee-oh-i-oo!
Surf?
Tow?
Or the wind?
Which of the three will it be?
The surf will it bludgeon and beat me dead?
Or the tow drag me down to the ocean bed?
Or the wind wail a dirge above my head?
Zoom
Sh-wsh-wsh
Ee-oh-i-oo.

Don Blanding

ELEPHANT SONG

Tong! Tong! Tong-a-tong-a-tong
That is the rhythm of the elephant song,
As the big grey elephants shuffle along
To the sing-song singing of the old brass bells,
To the shrill harsh stridence of the mahout's yells,
To the shuff-shuff-shuffle of the great round feet,
The elephants are swinging down the village street.
A priest peers out from his white-washed cell
When he hears the ringing of the elephant bell.
A wild-eyed faquir flings a mumbling curse,
A baby peers from the arms of its nurse,
A cobra dances to a charmer's tune,
The incense wavers in the shrine of the moon,
The street dogs scamper, the children scurry,
A woman hum-hums as she fixes curry,
And the bells keep ringing like a distant gong.
Tong! Tong! Tong-a-tong-a-tong
The swing-along rhythm of the elephant song.
Tong! Tong! Tong-a-tong-a-long.

Don Blanding

SONG OF THE FOX

To-morrow the fox will come to town,
    Keep, keep, keep, keep, keep,
To-morrow the fox will come to town,
    O keep you all well there.
I must desire you, neighbours all,
To hallo the fox out of the hall,
And cry as loud as you can call,
    Whoop, whoop, whoop, whoop, whoop.

He'll steal the Cock out from his flock,
    Keep, keep, keep, keep, keep,
He'll steal the Cock from out his flock,
    O keep you all well there.
I must desire you . . . *etc.*

He'll steal the Hen from out of the pen,
    Keep, keep, keep, keep, keep,
He'll steal the Hen out of the pen,
    O keep you all well there.
I must desire you . . . *etc.*

He'll steal the Duck out of the brook,
    Keep, keep, keep, keep, keep,
He'll steal the Duck out of the brook,
    O keep you all well there.
I must desire you . . . . *etc.*

He'll steal the Lamb even from his dam,
    Keep, keep, keep, keep, keep,
He'll steal the Lamb even from his dam,
    O keep you all well there.
I must desire you, neighbours all,
To hallo the fox out of the hall,
And cry as loud as you can call,
    Whoop, whoop, whoop, whoop, whoop.

Traditional

THE HUNT IS UP

The hunt is up,
The hunt is up,
And it is well nigh day;
And Harry our King
Has gone hunting
To bring his deer to bay.

The East is bright
With morning light,
And darkness it is fled:
The merry horn
Wakes up the morn
To leave his idle bed.

Awake, all men,
I say again,
Be merry as you may,
For Harry our King
Has gone hunting
To bring his deer to bay.

Sixteenth Century Song

A CARRION CROW

A carrion crow sat on an oak,
    Fol de riddle, lol de riddle, hi ding do,
Watching a tailor shape his cloak;
    Sing heigh-ho, the carrion crow,
    Fol de riddle, lol de riddle, hi ding do.

Wife, bring me my old bent bow,
    Fol de riddle, lol de riddle, hi ding do,
That I may shoot yon carrion crow;
    Sing heigh ho, the carrion crow,
    Fol de riddle, lol de riddle, hi ding do.

The tailor he shot and missed his mark,
    Fol de riddle, lol de riddle, hi ding do,
And shot his own sow quite through the heart;
    Sing heigh ho, the carrion crow,
    Fol de riddle, lol de riddle, hi ding do.

Wife, bring brandy in a spoon,
    Fol de riddle, lol de riddle, hi ding do,
For our old sow is in a swoon;
    Sing heigh ho, the carrion crow,
    Fol de riddle, lol de riddle, hi ding do.

Folk Song

THE MAKER OF CRADLES

He makes little cradles of fine lacquered wood,
He paints them with dragons and stars and birds,
They are carven and coloured and lined with silk,
And he weaves a charm for them to woven words.

("Where shall I rest your little tired head?
Son of my heart, lie still," she said.)

He makes little cradles of beaten bronze;
As light as a leaf is the fretted screen;
The pillow is scented with jasmine flowers,
The silken blanket is fit for a queen.

("Where shall I rest your tired little head?
Son of my heart, lie still," she said.)

He makes little cradles of silver and gold,
Turquoise and ivory gem the hood.
They swing from a peacock's outspread tail,
And the rockers are carved of sandal-wood.

("Where shall I rest your tired little head?
Son of my heart, lie still," she said.)

The gypsy mother goes humbly by,
The babe in her arms lies warm and still,
Oh, Maker of Cradles, you cannot weave
A lovelier cradle, for all your skill.

("Where shall I rest your little tired head?
Son of my heart, lie still," she said.)

Thora Stowell

BOUND TO CALIFORNIA

Goodbye, my lads, goodbye,
No one can tell me why
I am bound to California
To reap the shining gold!
Goodbye, my lads, goodbye,
No one can tell me why I
am bound to California
To reap the shining gold!

Sea Shanty

A WANDERER'S SONG

A wind's in the heart of me, a fire's in my heels,
I am tired of brick and stone and rumbling wagon-wheels;
I hunger for the sea's edge, the limits of the land.
Where the wild old Atlantic is shouting on the sand.

Oh, I'll be going, leaving the noises of the street,
To where a lifting foresail-foot is yanking at the sheet;
To a windy, tossing anchorage where yawls and ketches ride,
Oh I'll be going, going, until I meet the tide.

And first I'll hear the sea-wind, the mewing of the gulls,
The clucking, sucking of the sea about the rusty hulls,
The songs at the capstan in the hooker warping out,
And then the heart of me'll know I'm there or thereabout.

Oh I'm tired of brick and stone, the heart of me is sick,
For windy green, unquiet sea, the realm of Moby Dick;
And I'll be going, going, from the roaring of the wheels,
For a wind's in the heart of me, a fire's in my heels.

John Masefield

MERRY ARE THE BELLS

Merry are the bells, and merry would they ring,
Merry was myself, and merry could I sing;
With a merry ding-dong, happy, gay, and free,
And a merry sing-song, happy let us be!

Waddle goes your gait, and hollow are your hose;
Noddle goes your pate, and purple is your nose;
Merry is your sing-song, happy, gay, and free;
With a merry ding-dong, happy let us be!

Merry have we met, and merry have we been;
Merry let us part, and merry meet again;
With our merry sing-song, happy, gay, and free,
With a merry ding-dong, happy let us be!
Anon.

A FOX JUMPED UP

A fox jumped up on a moonlight night,
The stars were shining and all things bright:
"Oh, oh!" said the fox, "it's a very fine night
For me to go through the town, heigho!"

The fox when he came to yonder stile,
He lifted his ears, and he listened awhile;
"Oh, oh!" said the fox, "'tis but a short mile
From this to yonder town, heigho!"

The fox, when he came to the farmer's gate,
Whom should he see but the farmer's drake?
"I love you too well for your master's sake,

And I long to be picking your bones, heigho!"
The grey goose she ran round the hay-stack,
"Oh, oh!" said the fox, "you are very fat,
And you'll do very well to ride on my back
From this to yonder town, heigho!"

The farmer's wife she jumped out of bed,
And out of the window she popped her head,
And she cried, "Oh, husband! the geese are all dead,
For the fox has been through the town, heigho!"

The farmer loaded his pistol with lead,
And shot the old rogue of a fox through the head,
"Ah, ah!" said the farmer, "I think you are dead,
And no more will you trouble the town, heigho!"

Old Rhyme

PIPER PLAY!

Now the furnaces are out,
    And the aching anvils sleep;
Down the road the grimy rout
    Tramples homeward, twenty deep.
    Piper play! Piper play!
    Though we be o'erlaboured men,
Ripe for rest, pipe your best!
    Let us foot it once again!

Bridled looms delay their din;
    All the humming wheels are spent;
Busy spindles cease to spin;
    Warp and woof must rest content.

Piper play! Piper play!
   For a little we are free!
Foot it, girls, and shake your curls,
   Haggard creatures though we be!

Racked and soiled the faded air
   Freshens in our holiday;
Clouds and tides our respite share;
   Breezes linger by the way.
   Piper rest! Piper rest!
     Now, a carol of the moon!
   Piper, piper, play your best!
     Melt the sun into your tune!

Nameless as the stars of night
   Far in galaxies unfurled,
Yet we wield unrivalled might,
   Joints and hinges of the world!
   Night and day! Night and day!
     Sound the song the hours rehearse!
Work and play! work and play!
     The order of the universe!

Now the furnaces are out,
   And the aching anvils sleep;
Down the road a merry rout
   Dances homeward, twenty deep.
   Piper play! Piper play!
     Wearied people though we be,
Ripe for rest, pipe your best!
   For a little we are free!

John Davidson

THE CROCODILE

Now listen, you landsmen, unto me, to tell you the truth I'm bound.
What happened to me by going to sea, and the wonders that I found;
Shipwrecked I was once off Perouse and cast upon the shore.
So then I did resolve to roam, the country to explore.
    To my rit fal lal li bollem, to my rit fal lal li dee!
    To my rit fal lal li bollem, to my rit fal lal li dee!

'Twas far I had not started out, when close alongside the ocean,
I saw something move which at first I thought was all the world in motion;
But steering up close alongside, I found 'twas a crocodile,
And from his nose to the tip of his tail he measured five hundred mile.
    To my rit, etc.

While up aloft the wind was high, it blew a gale from the south,
I lost my hold and away did fly right into the crocodile's mouth,
He quickly closed his jaws on me and thought he'd got a victim,

But I ran down his throat, d'ye see, and that's the way I tricked him.
    To my rit, etc.

I travelled on for a month or two, till I got into his maw,
Where I found of rum kegs not a few, and a thousand fat bullocks in store,
Of life I banished all my care, for of grub I was not stinted.
And in this crocodile I lived ten years, and very well contented.
    To my rit, etc.

This crocodile being very old, one day, alas, he died;
He was ten long years a-getting cold, he was so long and wide.
His skin was eight miles thick, I'm sure, or very near about,
For I was full ten years or more a-cutting my way out.
    To my rit, etc.

And now I've once more got on earth, I've vowed no more to roam,
In a ship that passed I got a berth, and now I'm safe at home.
And if my story you should doubt, should you ever travel the Nile,
It's ten to one you'll find the shell of that wonderful crocodile.
    To my rit fal lal li bollem, to my rit fal lal li dee!

Folk Song

SIC VITA

Like to an eye which sleep doth chain;
Or like a star whose fall we feign;
Or like a shade on Ahaz' watch;
Or like a wave which gulfs do snatch;
Or like a wind or flame that's past;
Or smother'd news confirm'd at last;
Even so man's life, pawn'd in the grave,
Waits for a rising it must have.
   The eye still sees; the star still blazeth;
   The shade goes back; the wave escapeth;
   The wind is turn'd, the flame reviv'd;
   The news renew'd; and man new liv'd.

William Strode

SIC VITA

Like to a silkworm of one year;
Or like a wronged lover's tear;
Or on the waves a rudder's dint;
Or like the sparkles of a glint;
Or like to little cakes perfum'd;
Or fireworks made to be consum'd;
Even such is man, and all that trust
In weak and animated dust.
The silkworm droops; the tears soon shed;
The ship's way lost; the sparkle dead;
The cake is burnt; the firework done;
And man as these as quickly gone.

William Browne

WHEN BEGGARS RIDE

They say that every wish of ours
Adds one more feather to the wings
That lift us out of this grey world
Into the realm of fairy things.
And there, where every wish comes true,
Wishes are horses, winged and fine;
So even beggars there can ride—
I only wish such steeds were mine!

O Dearest Dear, I'd ride with you
Beyond the moon, beyond the sun;
We'd pick the stars to crown your hair,
And chase the comets, and we'd run
A-gallop up the Milky Way,
And drain the Dawn's enchanted wine,
O Dearest Dear, how far we'd stray,
If such fine steeds were yours and mine!

We'd climb the stately Pyramids
And see the splendours of old Rome,
And cherry blossom in Japan,
And pale Niagara's crown of foam,
And moonlight glories of the Taj,
And Southern Seas whose islands shine
Like fairy dreams—if it were true
That such fine steeds were yours and mine.
   But Dearest Dear we're beggars yet,
   Except when, dreaming, we forget.

Thora Stowell

THE FROG AND THE CROW

A jolly fat frog did in the river swim, O.
A comely black crow lived on the river brim, O.
"Come on shore, come on shore," said the crow to the frog, and then, O,
"No, you'll bite me; no, you'll bite me," said the frog to the crow again, O.

"Oh, there is sweet music on yonder green hill, O,
And you shall be a dancer, a dancer in yellow.
All in yellow, all in yellow," said the crow to the frog, and then, O,
"All in yellow, all in yellow," said the frog to the crow again, O.

"Farewell, ye little fishes, that in the river swim, O.
I go to be a dancer, a dancer in yellow."
"Oh beware; oh beware," said the fish to the frog and then, O.
"I'll take care, I'll take care," said the frog to the fish again, O.

The frog began a-swimming, a-swimming to land, O.
The crow began a-hopping to give him his hand, O.
"Sir, you're welcome; sir, you're welcome," said the crow to
    the frog, and then, O,
"Sir, I thank you; sir, I thank you," said the frog to the crow
    again, O.

"But where is the music on yonder green hill, O?
And where are all the dancers, the dancers in yellow?
All in yellow, all in yellow," said the frog to the crow, and
    then, O—
But he chuckled, oh he chuckled, and then, O, and then, O!

Anon.

CASEY JONES

Come all you rounders if you want to hear
The story of a brave engineer;
Casey Jones was the hogger's name,
On a big eight-wheeler, boys, he won his fame.
Caller called Casey at half-past four,
He kissed his wife at the station door,
Mounted to his cabin with orders in his hand,
And took his farewell trip to the promised land.

> Casey Jones, he mounted to the cabin,
> Casey Jones, with his orders in his hand!
> Casey Jones, he mounted to the cabin,
> Took his farewell trip into the promised land.

Put in your water and shovel in your coal,
Put your head out of the window, watch the drivers roll,
I'll run her till she leaves the rail,
'Cause we're eight hours late with the Western Mail!
He looked at his watch and his watch was slow,
Looked at the water and the water was low,
Turned to the fireboy and said,
"We'll get to 'Frisco, but we'll all be dead!"

> Casey Jones, he mounted to the cabin,
> Casey Jones, with his orders in his hand!
> Casey Jones, he mounted to the cabin,
> Took his farewell trip into the promised land.

Casey pulled up Reno Hill,
Tooted for the crossing like a whippoorwill,
Snakes all knew by the engine's moans
That the hogger at the throttle was Casey Jones.
He pulled up short two miles from the place,
Number Four stared him right in the face,
Turned to his fireboy, said, "You'd better jump,
'Cause there's two locomotives that's going to bump!"

    Casey Jones, he mounted to the cabin,
    Casey Jones, with his orders in his hand!
    Casey Jones, he mounted to the cabin,
    Took his farewell trip into the promised land.

Casey said, just before he died,
"There's two more roads I'd like to ride."
Fireboy said, "What can they be?"
"The Aitchison-Topeka and the Santa Fe."
Mrs Jones sat on her bed a-sighing,
Got a pink that Casey was dying,
Said, "Go to bed, children; hush your crying,
'Cause you'll get another papa on the Salt Lake line."

    Casey Jones! Got another papa!
    Casey Jones, on the Salt Lake line!
    Casey Jones! Got another papa!
    Got another papa on the Salt Lake line.

Old American Ballad

A NAUGHTY BOY
(From *A Song About Myself*)

There was a naughty boy,
    And a naughty boy was he,
He ran away to Scotland,
    The people there to see—
    Then he found
    That the ground
    Was as hard,
    That a yard,
    Was as long,
    That a song,
    Was as merry,
    That a cherry,
    Was as red,
    That lead,
    Was as weighty,
    That fourscore,
    Was as eighty,
    That a door,
    Was as wooden,
    As in England—
So he stood in his shoes
    And he wondered,
    He wondered,
He stood in his shoes
    And he wondered.

John Keats

YE SPOTTED SNAKES

Ye spotted snakes with double tongue,
   Thorny hedgehogs be not seen;
Newts and blind-worms, do no wrong;
   Come not near our fairy queen.

   Philomel with melody,
   Sing in our sweet lullaby;
Lulla, lulla, lullaby; lulla, lulla, lullaby!
   Never harm,
   Nor spell nor charm,
Come our lovely lady nigh;
So good night, with lullaby.

Weaving spiders, come not near;
   Hence, you long-legged spinners hence!
Beetles black, approach not near;
   Worm nor snail, do no offence.

   Philomel with melody,
   Sing in our sweet lullaby;
Lulla, lulla, lullaby; lulla, lulla, lullaby!
   Never harm,
   Nor spell nor charm,
Come our lovely lady nigh;
So good-night, with lullaby.

William Shakespeare

THE ONE-EYED RILEY

As I was sitting by the fire,
   Talking to old Riley's daughter,
Suddenly a thought came into my head,
   I'd like to marry old Riley's daughter.

      Giddy-i-ay, giddy-i-ay,
      Giddy-i-ay to the one-eyed Riley.
      Bom bom bom! Bom bom bom!
      Try it on your old bass drum.

For Riley played on the big bass drum,
   Riley had a mind for murdering slaughter,
Riley had a bright red glittering eye
   And he kept that eye on his lovely daughter.
      Giddy-i-ay . . .

Her hair was black and her eyes were blue:
   The Colonel and the Major and the Captain sought her,
The Sergeant and the private and the drummer boy too,
   But they never had a chance with Riley's daughter.
      Giddy-i-ay . . .

I got me a ring and a parson too,
   I got me a scratch in the married quarter,
Settled me down to a peaceful life,
   As happy as a king with Riley's daughter.
      Giddy-i-ay . . .

Suddenly a footstep on the stair—
   Who should it be but the one-eyed Riley,
With two pistols in his hand,
   Looking for the man who had married his daughter!

  Giddy-i-ay . . .
I took old Riley by the hair,
  Rammed his head in a pail of water,
Fired his pistols into the air,
  A darned sight quicker than I married his daughter!

  Giddy-i-ay, giddy-i-ay,
  Giddy-i-ay to the one-eyed Riley,
  Bom bom bom! Bom bom bom!
  Try it on your old bass drum.

Anon.

BATTLE SONG (From *The Mad Lover*)

Arm, arm, arm, arm! The scouts are all come in,
Keep your ranks close, and now your honours win.
Behold from yonder hill the foe appears;
Bows, bills, glaves, arrows, shields, and spears;
Like a dark wood he comes, or tempest pouring;
Oh, view the wings of horse the meadows scouring!
The van-guard marches bravely.
Hark, the drums,
 Dub, dub!

They meet, they meet! Now the battle comes:
 See how the arrows fly,
 That darken all the sky;
 Hark how the trumpets sound,
 Hark how the hills rebound!
 Tara, tara, tara, tara!

Hark how the horses charge! In boys, boys, in!
The battle totters; now the wounds begin;
    Oh, how they cry,
    Oh, how they die!
Room for the valiant Memnon arm'd with thunder!
    See how he breaks the ranks asunder.

They fly, they fly! Eumenes has the chase,
And brave Polybius makes good his place.
    To the plains, to the woods,
    To the rocks, to the floods,
They fly for succour. Follow, follow, follow!

Hark how the soldiers hollo!
    Hey, hey,
Brave Diocles is dead,
And all his soldiers fled,
The battle's won and lost,
That many a life has cost.

John Fletcher

THE SHEPHERD BOY AND THE WOLF

A shepherd boy beside a stream
"The wolf, the wolf!" was wont to scream,
And when the villagers appeared,
He'd laugh and call them silly-eared.

A wolf at last came down the steep—
"The wolf, the wolf!—My legs, my sheep!"
The creature had a jolly feast,
Quite undisturbed, on boy and beast.

For none believes the liar, forsooth,
Even when the liar speaks the truth.

From Æsop

THE GENTLEMAN ON THE GATE

And now if e'er by chance I put my fingers into glue,
Or madly squeeze a right-hand foot into a left-hand shoe,
Or if I drop upon my toe a very heavy weight,
I weep, for it reminds me so
Of that old man I used to know—
Whose look was mild, whose speech was slow,
Whose hair was whiter than the snow,
Whose face was very like a crow,
With eyes, like cinders, all aglow,
Who seemed distracted with his woe,
Who rocked his body to and fro,
And muttered mumblingly and low,
As if his mouth were full of dough,
Who snorted like a buffalo—
That summer evening long ago
A-sitting on a gate.

Lewis Carroll

Part Two

Pictures in Poetry

THE RIDE-BY-NIGHTS

Upon their brooms the Witches stream,
Crooked and black in the crescent's gleam;
One foot high, and one foot low,
Bearded, cloaked, and cowled, they go.
Neath Charlie's Wain they twitter and tweet,
And away they swarm 'neath the Dragon's feet.
With a whoop and a flutter they swing and sway,
And surge pell-mell down the Milky Way.
Between the legs of the glittering Chair
They hover and squeak in the empty air.
Then round they swoop past the glimmering Lion
To where Sirius barks behind huge Orion;
Up, then, and over to wheel amain,
Under the silver, and home again.

Walter De La Mare

NIGHT SONG IN THE JUNGLE

Now Rann the Kite brings home the night
    That Mang the Bat sets free—
The herds are shut in byre and hut,
    For loosed till dawn are we.
This is the hour of pride and power,
    Talon and tusk and claw.
Oh hear the call!—Good hunting all
    That keep the Jungle law!

Rudyard Kipling

From THE GARDENER

Over the green and yellow rice-fields sweep the shadows of
   the autumn clouds followed by the swift chasing sun.
The bees forget to sip their honey; drunken with light they
   foolishly hover and hum.
The ducks in the islands of the river clamour in joy for mere
   nothing.
Let none go back home, brothers, this morning, let none go to
   work.
Let us take the blue sky by storm and plunder space as we run.
   Laughter floats in the air like foam on the flood.
   Brother, let us squander our morning, our morning in futile
songs.

Rabindranath Tagore

LO-YANG

A beautiful place is the town of Lo-Yang;
The big streets are full of spring light.
The lads go driving out with harps in their hands:
The mulberry girls go out of the fields with their baskets.
Gold whips glint at the horses' flanks,
Gauze sleeves brush the green boughs.
Racing dawn, the carriages come home—
And the girls with their high baskets full of fruit.

Arthur Waley

THREE YOUNG RATS

Three young rats with black felt hats,
Three young ducks with white straw flats.
Three young dogs with curling tails,
Three young cats with demi-veils,
Went out to walk with three young pigs
In satin vests and sorrel wigs.
But suddenly it chanced to rain,
And so they all went home again.

Anon.

AMPHIBIAN

The fancy I had today,
    Fancy which turned out a fear!
I swam far out in the bay,
    Since waves laughed warm and clear.

I lay and looked at the sun,
    The noon-sun looked at me:
Between us two, no one
    Live creature, that I could see.

Yes! There came floating by
    Me, who lay floating too,
Such a strange butterfly!
    Creature as dear as new:

Because the membraned wings
    So wonderful, so wide,
So sun-suffused, were things
    Like soul and naught beside.

A handbreadth over head!
    All of the sea my own,
It owned the sky instead;
    Both of us were alone.

Robert Browning

IF

If all the world were paper,
And all the sea were ink,
If all the trees were bread and cheese,
How should we do for drink?

If all the world were sand'o,
Oh then what should we lack'o;
If as they say there were no clay;
How should we take tobacco?

If all our vessels ran'a,
If none but had a crack'a;
If Spanish apes ate all the grapes,
How should we do for sack'a?

If friars had no bald pates,
Nor nuns had no dark cloisters;
If all the seas were beans and peas,
How should we do for oysters?

If there had been no projects,
Nor none that did great wrongs.
If fiddlers still turn players all,
How should we do for songs?

If all things were eternal,
And nothing their end bringing;
If this should be, then how should we,
Here make an end of singing?

Anon.

From EVENING

The great rain is over,
    The little rain begun
Falling from the higher leaves,
    Bright in the sun,
Down to the lower leaves,
    One drop by one.

Mary Coleridge

THE COMMON CORMORANT

The Common Cormorant or shag
Lays eggs inside a paper bag.
The reason you will see no doubt
Is to keep the lightning out.
But what these unobservant birds
Have never noticed is that herds
Of wandering bears may come with buns
And steal the bags to hold the crumbs.

Anon.

THE SNAIL

To grass, or leaf, or fruit, or wall,
The Snail sticks close, nor fears to fall,
As if he grew there, house and all
        Together.

Within that house secure he hides,
When danger imminent betides
Of storms, or other harm besides,
        Of weather.

Give but his horns the slightest touch,
His self-collecting power is such,
He shrinks into his house with much
        Displeasure.

Where'er he dwells, he dwells alone,
Except himself has chattels none,
Well satisfied to be his own
        Whole treasure.

Thus hermit-like, his life he leads,
Nor partner of his Banquet needs,
And if he meets one, only feeds
        The faster.

Who seeks him must be worse than blind
(He and his house are so combined)
If, finding it, he fails to find
        Its master.

William Cowper

SNAKE

A narrow fellow in the grass
Occasionally rides;
You may have met him—did you not?
His notice sudden is.

The grass divides as with a comb,
A spotted shaft is seen;
And then it closes at your feet
And opens further on.

He likes a boggy acre,
A floor too cool for corn.
Yet when a child, and barefoot,
I more than once, at morn,

Have passed, I thought, a whip-lash
Unbraiding in the sun—
When, stopping to secure it,
It wrinkled, and was gone.

Several of nature's people
I know, and they know me;
I feel for them a transport
Of cordiality;

But never met this fellow,
Attended or alone,
Without a tighter breathing,
And zero at the bone.

Emily Dickinson

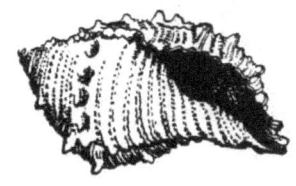

THE SHELL

See what a lovely shell,
Small and pure as a pearl,
Lying close to my foot,
Frail, but a work divine,
Made so fairly well
With delicate spire and whorl,
How exquisitely minute,
A miracle of design!

What is it? a learned man
Could give it a clumsy name.
Let him name it who can,
The beauty would be the same.

The tiny cell is forlorn,
Void of the little living will
That made it stir on the shore.
Did he stand at the diamond door
Of his house in a rainbow frill?
Did he push, when he was uncurl'd,
A golden foot or fairy horn
Thro' his dim water-world?

Slight, to be crushed with a tap
Of my finger-nail on the sand;
Small, but a work divine,
Frail, but of force to withstand,
Year upon year, the shock
Of cataract seas that snap
The three-decker's oaken spine
Athwart the ledges of rock,
Here on the Breton strand!

Alfred, Lord Tennyson

THE POULTRIES

Let's think of eggs.
They have no legs.
Chickens come from eggs
But they have legs. The plot thickens;
Eggs come from chickens,
But have no legs under 'em.
What a conundrum!

Ogden Nash

THE WIND IN THE GRASS

The green grass is bowing,
The morning wind is in it,
'Tis a tune worth thy knowing,
Though it change every minute.

Ralph W. Emerson

VIGIL

I watch the good ships on the sea,
Yet never ship comes home to me.

Out of the crowded ports they sail
To crowded ports that cry them hail.

And still they bring no word to me,
Tall-masted ships upon the sea.

As gallant messengers they go
Laughing against all winds that blow.

Yet never ship upon the sea
Bears blessed merchandise for me.

I watch them pass from friend to friend
All day from world's end to world's end.

No pleasant ship comes down to me
Along the long leagues of the sea.

Nor sign nor salutation made,
Beyond the far sea-line they fade.

Yet as I watch them on the sea
All ships are piloted by me.

John Drinkwater

A PIPER

A piper in the streets to-day
Set up and tuned, and started to play,
And away, away, away on the tide
Of his music we started; on every side
Doors and windows were opened wide,
And men left down their work and came,
And women with petticoats coloured like flame,
And little bare feet that were blue with cold,
Went dancing back to the age of gold,
And all the world went gay, went gay,
For half-an-hour in the street to-day.

Seumas O'Sullivan

THE ISLAND

If I had a ship,
I'd sail my ship,
I'd sail my ship,
Through Eastern seas;
Down to a beach where the slow
waves thunder—
The green curls over and the white
falls under—
Boom! Boom! Boom!
On the sun-bright sand.
Then I'd leave my ship and I'd land,
And climb the steep white sand.

And climb to the trees,
The six dark trees,
The coco-nut trees on the cliff's green crown—
Hands and knees
To the coco-nut trees,
Face to the cliff as the stones patter down,
Up, up, up, staggering, stumbling,
Round the corner where the rock is crumbling,
Round this shoulder,
Over this boulder,
Up to the top where the six trees stand . . ..

And there I would rest, and lie,
My chin in my hands, and gaze
At the dazzle of sand below,
And the green waves curling slow,
And the grey-blue distant haze
Where the sea goes up to the sky . . ..

And I'd say to myself as I looked so lazily down at the sea:
"There's nobody else in the world, and the World was made for
   me."

A. A. Milne

THE HOUSEKEEPER

The frugal snail, with forecast of repose,
Carries his house with him wher'er he goes;
Peeps out—and if there comes a shower of rain,
Retreats to his small domicile again.
Touch but a tip of him, a horn—'tis well—
He curls up in his sanctuary shell.
He's his own landlord, his own tenant; stay
Long as he will, he dreads no Quarter Day.
Himself he boards and lodges; both invites
And feasts himself; sleeps with himself o'nights.
He spares the upholsterer trouble to procure
Chattels; himself is his own furniture,
And his sole riches. Whereso'er he roam—
Knock when you will—he's sure to be at home.

Charles Lamb

ROMANCE

When I was but thirteen or so
I went into a golden land,
Chimborazo, Cotopaxi
Took me by the hand.

My father died, my brother too,
They passed like fleeting dreams.
I stood where Popocatapetl
In the sunlight gleams.

I dimly heard the master's voice
And boys far-off at play,
Chimborazo, Cotopaxi
Had stolen me away.

I walked in a great golden dream
To and fro from school—
Shining Popocatapetl
The dusty streets did rule.

I walked home with a gold dark boy,
And never a word I'd say,
Chimborazo, Cotopaxi
Had taken my speech away.

I gazed entranced upon his face
Fairer than any flower—
O shining Popocatapetl
It was thy magic hour:

The houses, people, traffic seemed
Thin fading dreams by day,
Chimborazo, Cotopaxi
They had stolen my soul away!

W. J. Turner

THE LION'S SKELETON

How long, O lion, hast thou fleshless lain?
What rapt thy fierce and thirsty eyes away?
First came the vulture: worms, heat, wind, and rain
Ensued, and ardours of the tropic day.
I know not—if they spared it thee—how long
The canker sate within thy monstrous mane,
Till it fell piecemeal and bestrew'd the plain;
Or, shredded by the storming sands, was flung
Again to earth; but now thine ample front,
Whereon the great frowns gather'd, is laid bare;
The thunders of thy throat, which erst were wont
To scare the desert, are no longer there;
Thy claws remain, but worms, wind, rain, and heat
Have sifted out the substance of thy feet.

Charles Tennyson-Turner

THE BRIDGE

Here, with one leap,
The bridge that spans the cutting; on its back The load
Of the main-road,
And under it the railway track.
    Into the plains they sweep,
    Into the solitary plains asleep,
    The flowing lines, the parallel lines of steel—
    Into the plains they pass,
    The flowing lines, like arms of mute appeal.

A cry
Prolonged across the earth—a call
To the remote horizons and the sky;

The whole east rushes down them with its light,
And the whole west receives them, with its pall
Of stars and night—
The flowing lines, the parallel lines of steel.
And with the fall of darkness,
See! the red,
Bright anger of the signal, where it flares
Like a huge eye that stares
On some hid danger in the dark ahead.
A twang of wire—unseen
The signal drops; and now, instead
Of a red eye, a green.

Out of the silence grows
An iron thunder—grows and roars, and sweeps,
Menacing! The plain
Suddenly leaps,
Startled, from its repose—
Alert and listening. Now, from the gloom
Of the soft distance, loom
Three lights and, over them, a brush
Of tawny flame, and flying spark—
Three pointed lights that rush,
Monstrous, upon the cringing dark.

And nearer, nearer rolls the sound,
Louder the throb and roar of wheels,
The shout of speed, the shriek of steam;
The sloping bank,
Cut into flashing squares, gives back the clank
And grind of metal, while the ground
Shudders and the bridge reels—
As, with a scream,
The train,
A rage of smoke, a laugh of fire,
A lighted anguish of desire,
A dream
Of gold and iron, of sound and flight,
Tumultuous roars across the night.

The train roars past—and, with a cry,
Drowned in a flying howl of wind,
Half-stifled in the smoke and blind,
The plain,
Shaken, exultant, unconfined,
Rises, flows on, and follows, and sweeps by,
Shrieking, to lose itself in distance and the sky.
J. Redwood Anderson

THE OLD STONE HOUSE
Nothing on the grey roof, nothing on the brown,
Only a little greening where the rain drips down;
Nobody at the window, nobody at the door,
Only a little hollow which a foot once wore;
But still I tread on tiptoe, still tiptoe on I go,
Past nettles, porch, and weedy well, for oh, I know
A friendless face is peering, and a clear still eye
Peeps closely through the casement as my step goes by.
Walter De La Mare

I LIKE TO SEE . . .

I like to see it lap up the miles,
And lick the valleys up,
And stop to feed itself at tanks;
And then, prodigious, step

Around a pile of mountains,
And, supercilious, peer
In shanties by the sides of roads;
And then a quarry pare

To fit its sides, and crawl between
Complaining all the while
In horrid, hooting stanza;
Then chase itself downhill

And neigh like Boanerges;
Then, punctual as a star,
Stop docile and omnipotent—
At its own stable door.

Emily Dickinson

THE CANE-BOTTOM'D CHAIR

In tattered old slippers that toast at the bars,
And a ragged old jacket perfumed with cigars,
Away from the world and its toils and its cares,
I've a snug little kingdom up four pair of stairs.

To mount to this realm is a toil to be sure,
But the fire there is bright and the air rather pure;

And the view I behold on a sunshiny day
Is grand, through the chimney pots over the way.

This snug little chamber is crammed in all nooks
With worthless old knicknacks and silly old books,
And foolish old odds and foolish old ends,
Crack'd bargains from brokers, cheap keepsakes from friends.

Old armour, prints, pictures, pipes, china (all crack'd),
Old rickety tables, and chairs broken-backed;
A twopenny treasure, wondrous to see;
What matter? 'tis pleasant to you, friend, and me.

No better divan need the Sultan require,
Than the creaking old sofa that basks by the fire;
And 'tis wonderful, surely, what music you get
From the rickety, ramshackle, wheezy spinet.

That praying-rug came from a Turkoman's camp;
By Tiber once twinkled that brazen old lamp;
A Mameluke fierce yonder dagger has drawn:
'Tis a murderous knife to toast muffins upon.

Long, long through the hours, and the night, and the chimes,
Here we talk of old books, and old friends, and old times;
As we sit in a fog made of rich Latakie,
This chamber is pleasant to you, friend, and me.

But of all the cheap treasures that garnish my nest,
There's one that I love and I cherish the best;
For the finest of couches that's padded with hair
I never would change thee, my cane-bottom'd chair. . ..

W. M. Thackeray

IN THE JUNGLE

Here through the sea-green twilight slinks
    The tiger with his jewelled eye,
And sleek and slim the crafty lynx,
    Prick-eared, like Satan, lurches by.
The lion, ruffed in kingly gold,
    Awakes and stretches in his lair;
Bright birds, like fiery meteors, scold
    Fluttering through the sunless air;
And through the spawning undergrowth
    The bronze-bright snake, flat-headed, keen,
Wakened from a month of sloth
    Flows on his rustling way unseen.
Here like a vast unburied root
    The river-horse sleeps in the ooze,
And poisonous flowers and fatal fruit
    Drip from above their deadly dews.

But hid beneath the tiger's stealth,
    The lion's rage, the lynx's guile,
Behind the teeming poisonous wealth
    Of flower and fruit—older than Nile,
Craftier than palaces of popes
    And crueller than Spanish kings,
The Jungle Spirit grins and gropes,
    Snaring in stealthy-footed rings
The traveller, whose mazed sight
    Shall never greet his native groves,
Nor ever find the sweet daylight,
    Nor see again the face he loves.

Martin Armstrong

THE MALAY KRIS

Mid the blade was damask fateful,
Setting foe's allotted span,
And at point the lam and alif
Seen by Muslims when they're dying.
Of no common steel 'twas fashioned,
Forged of fragments of the metal
Used for bolt on Mecca's Kaabah . . .
Burnished 'twas with fragrant water,
In a furnace brought from China.
Should you clean the kris with acid
In the river's upper reaches,
Dead the fish at mouth of river.

Sir Richard Winstedt

PARACHUTE

He poises a moment and looks at the earth far under,
Featureless, small, and those steep miles between;
His spirit shrinks, but he grips and with closed eyes throws
Bodily outward, his breath is snatched up as he goes
Hurtling, a blunt weight, downward through a tense storm
Of air that numbs him with a dim drug of thunder
Till his being burns dazed as a windy spark. A pull
That lifts him to an abrupt stillness, and then
Thought clears, his body loosens, glides smooth as a gull
Through deepening calms with smells of the land warm:
The land that grows bright with returning green and gold,
Links, masses, and sets in its lines like ore in the mould;
Down to firm, century-anchored earth, to pace
In safety amid the treacheries of space.

Stanley Snaith

INDIA

They hunt, the velvet tigers in the jungle,
The spotted jungle full of shapeless patches—
Sometimes they're leaves, sometimes they're hanging flowers,
Sometimes they're hot gold patches of the sun:
They hunt, the velvet tigers in the jungle!

What do they hunt by glimmering pools of water,
By the round silver Moon, the Pool of Heaven?—
In the striped grass, amid the barkless trees—
The stars scattered like eyes of beasts above them!

What do they hunt, their hot breath scorching insects?
Insects that blunder blindly in the way,

Vividly fluttering—they also are hunting,
Are glittering with a tiny ecstasy!

The grass is flaming and the trees are growing,
The very mud is gurgling in the pools,
Green toads are watching, crimson parrots flying,
Two pairs of eyes meet one another glowing—
They hunt, the velvet tigers in the jungle.

W. J. Turner

CARGOES

Quinquereme of Nineveh from distant Ophir
Rowing home to haven in sunny Palestine,
   With a cargo of ivory,
   And apes and peacocks,
  Sandalwood, cedarwood, and sweet white wine.

Stately Spanish galleon coming from the Isthmus,
Dipping through the tropics by the palm-green shores,
   With a cargo of diamonds,
   Emeralds, amethysts,
Topazes, and cinnamon, and gold moidores.

Dirty British coaster with a salt-caked smokestack
Butting through the Channel in the mad March days,
   With a cargo of Tyne coal,
   Road rail, pig lead,
Firewood, ironware, and cheap tin trays.

John Masefield

DESERTED

The old house leans upon a tree
Like some old man upon a staff:
The night wind in its ancient porch
Sounds like a hollow laugh.

The heaven is wrapped in flying clouds
As grandeur cloaks itself in gray:
The starlight flitting in and out,
Glints like a lanthorn ray.

The dark is full of whispers. Now
A fox-hound howls: and through the night,
Like some old ghost from out its grave,
The moon comes misty white.

Madison Cawein

WITH SHIPS THE SEA WAS SPRINKLED

With ships the sea was sprinkled far and nigh,
Like stars in heaven, and joyously it showed;
Some lying fast at anchor in the road,
Some veering up and down, one knew not why.
A goodly vessel did I then espy
Come like a giant from a haven broad:
And lustily along the bay she strode,
Her tackling rich, and of apparel high.
This ship was nought to me nor I to her,
Yet I pursued her with a lover's look;
This ship to all the rest I did prefer:
When will she turn and whither? She will brook
No tarrying: where She comes the Winds must stir:
On went she, and due north her journey took.

William Wordsworth

Part Three

The Poet as Storyteller

THE HANGMAN'S TREE

Hangman, hangman, hold your hand,
    O hold it wide and far,
For yonder I see my father coming,
    Riding through the air.

"Father, father, have you brought me gold,
    Or have you paid my fee?
Or have you come to see me hung
    Beneath the hangman's tree?"

"I have not brought you gold,
    I have not paid your fee,
But I have come to see you hung
    Beneath the hangman's tree."

"Hangman, hangman, hold your hand,
    O hold it wide and far,
For yonder I see my mother coming,
    Riding through the air.

"Mother, mother, have you brought me gold,
    Or have you paid my fee?
Or have you come to see me hung,
    Beneath the hangman's tree?"

"I have not brought you gold,
    I have not paid your fee,
But I have come to see you hung
    Beneath the hangman's tree."

"Hangman, hangman, hold your hand,
   O hold it wide and far,
For yonder I see my sister coming,
   Riding through the air.

"Sister, sister, have you brought me gold,
   Or have you paid my fee?
Or have you come to see me hung
   Beneath the hangman's tree?"

"I have not brought you gold,
   I have not paid your fee,
But I have come to see you hung
   Beneath the hangman's tree."

"Hangman, hangman, hold your hand,
   O hold it wide and far,
For yonder I see my sweetheart coming,
   Riding through the air.

"Sweetheart, sweetheart, have you brought me gold,
   Or have you paid my fee?
Or have you come to see me hung
   Beneath the hangman's tree?"

"O I have brought you gold,
   And I have paid your fee,
And I have come to take you from
   Beneath the hangman's tree!"

Anon.

THE SLAVE'S DREAM

Beside the ungathered rice he lay,
   His sickle in his hand;
His breast was bare, his matted hair
   Was buried in the sand.
Again, in the mist and the shadow of sleep,
   He saw his native land.

Wide through the landscape of his dreams
   The lordly Niger flowed;
Beneath the palm-trees on the plain
   Once more a king he strode,
And heard the tinkling caravans
   Descend the mountain road.

He saw once more his dark-eyed queen
   Among her children stand;
They clasped his neck, they kissed his cheeks,
   They held him by the hand!—
A tear burst from the sleeper's lids
   And fell into the sand.

And then at furious speed he rode

Along the Niger's bank;
His bridle-reins were golden chains,
   And, with a martial clank,
At each leap he could feel his scabbard of steel
   Smiting his stallion's flank.

Before him, like a blood-red flag,
   The bright flamingoes flew;
From morn till night he followed their flight,
   O'er plains where the tamarind grew,
Till he saw the roofs of Caffre huts,
   And the ocean rose to view.

At night he heard the lion roar,
   And the hyena scream,
And the river-horse, as he crushed the reeds
   Beside some hidden stream;
And it passed, like a glorious roll of drums,
   Through the triumph of his dream.

The forests, with their myriad tongues,
   Shouted of liberty;
And the Blast of the Desert cried aloud,
   With a voice so wild and free,
That he started in his sleep and smiled
   At their tempestuous glee.

He did not feel the driver's whip,
   Nor the burning heat of day;
For Death had illuminated the Land of Sleep,
   And his lifeless body lay
A worn-out fetter, that the soul
   Had broken and thrown away.
H. W. Longfellow

THE TOWKAY

Long ago, I do remember,
At the turning of the year,
I walked by lakes of lotus,
Their waters prism-clear.

But now there is no magic
In lotus flowers or seeds,
In rustling fields of orchids,
Or windy, water-reeds;

But I have endless business
And problems everywhere,
So I can tread on lotus
And never see them there.

Margaret Leong

BALLAD
(From the novel, *Arthur Coningsby*)

A maiden came gliding o'er the sea
In a boat as light as boat could be,
And she sang in tones so sweet and free,
"O, where is the youth that will follow me?"

Her forehead was white as the pearly shell,
Her form was finer than tongue can tell,
Her bosom heaved with a gentle swell,
And her voice was a distant vesper-bell.

And she still sang, while the western light
Fell on her figure so soft and bright,

"O, where shall I find the brave young sprite
That will follow the track of my boat to-night?"

To the strand the youths of the village run,
When the witching song had scarce begun,
And ere the set of the evening's sun,
Fifteen bold lovers the maid has won.
They hoisted the sail, and they plied the oar,
And away they went from their native shore,
While the damsel's pinnace flew fast before,
But never, O never! we saw them more.

John Sterling

AN INCIDENT OF THE FRENCH CAMP

You know, we French stormed Ratisbon;
    A mile or so away,
On a little mound, Napoleon
    Stood on our storming day;
With neck out-thrust, you fancy how,
    Legs wide, arms locked behind,
As if to balance the prone brow
    Oppressive with its mind.

Just as perhaps he mused, "My plans
    That soar to earth may fall,
Let once my army-leader Lannes
    Waver at yonder wall."
Out 'twixt the battery smokes there flew
    A rider, bound on bound,
Full galloping; nor bridle drew
    Until he reached the mound.

Then off there flung in smiling joy,
    And held himself erect
By just his horse's mane, a boy:
    You hardly could suspect—
(So tight he kept his lips compressed,
    Scarce any blood came through!)—
You looked twice ere you saw his breast
    Was all but shot in two.

"Well," cried he, "Emperor, by God's grace
    We've got you Ratisbon!
The Marshal's in the market-place.
    And you'll be there anon
To see your flag-bird flap his vans,
    Where I, to heart's desire,
Perched him!" The chief's eye flashed, his plans
    Soared up again like fire.

The chief's eye flashed; but presently
    Softened itself, as sheathes
A film the mother eagle's eye

When her bruised eaglet breathes:
"You're wounded!" "Nay," the soldier's pride
　　Touched to the quick, he said:
"I'm killed, Sire!" And, his chief beside,
　　Smiling, the boy fell dead.

Robert Browning

THE GLOVE AND THE LIONS

King Francis was a hearty king and loved a royal sport,
And one day, as his lions fought, sat looking at the court;
The nobles fill'd the benches, and the ladies in their pride,
And 'mongst them sat the Count de Lorge, with one for whom
　　he sighed;
And truly 'twas a gallant thing to see that crowning show—
Valour, and love and a king above, and the royal beasts below.

Ramped and roared the lions, with horrid, laughing jaws; They
　　bit, they glared, gave blows like beams, a wind went with
　　their paws,
With wallowing might and stifled roar they rolled on one
another,
Till all the pit with sand and mane was in a thunderous
　　smother;
The bloody foam above the bars came whistling through the
　　air;
Said Francis then, "Faith, gentlemen, we're better here than
　　there!"

De Lorge's love o'erheard the King, a beauteous, lively dame,
With smiling lips, and sharp, bright, eyes, which always
   seemed the same;
She thought, "The Count, my lover, is brave as brave can be,
He surely would do wondrous things to show his love of me;
King, ladies, lovers, all look on, the occasion is divine;
I'll drop my glove to prove his love; great glory will be mine."

She dropped her glove to prove his love, then looked at him
   and smiled;
He bowed, and in a moment leaped among the lions wild;
The leap was quick, return was quick; he has regained his
   place,
Then threw the glove, but not with love, right in the lady's
   face!
"By Heavens!" said Francis, "rightly done!" and he rose from
   where he sat
"No love, quoth he, "but vanity sets love a task like that."

Leigh Hunt

THE KNIGHT'S LEAP

"So the foemen have fired the gate, men of mine;
And the water is spent and gone?
Then bring me a cup of the red Ahr-wine:
    I never shall drink but this one.

"And reach me my harness, and saddle my horse,
And lead him me round to the door;
He must take such a leap to-night perforce
    As horse never took before. .

"I have fought my fight, I have lived my life,
I have drunk my share of wine;
From Trier to Coin there was never a knight
    Led a merrier life than mine.

"I have lived by the saddle for years two score;
And if I must die on tree,
Then the old saddle-tree, which has borne me of yore,
   Is the properest timber for me.

"So now to show bishop, and burgher, and priest
How the Altenahr hawk can die:
If they smoke the old falcon out of his nest,
   He must take to his wings and fly."

He harnessed himself by the clear moonshine,
And he mounted his horse at the door;
And he drained such a cup of the red Ahr-wine
   As man never drained before.

He spurred the old horse, and he held him tight,
And he leapt him out over the wall;
Out over the cliff, out into the night,
   Three hundred feet of fall.

They found him next morning below in the glen,
With never a bone in him whole—
A mass or a prayer now, good gentlemen,
   For such a brave rider's soul.

Charles Kingsley

PAUL REVERE'S RIDE

1
Listen, my children, and you shall hear
Of the midnight ride of Paul Revere,
On the eighteenth of April, in Seventy-five;
Hardly a man is now alive
Who remembers that famous day and year.

2
He said to his friend, "If the British march
By land or sea from the town tonight,
Hang a lantern aloft in the belfry arch
Of the North Church tower as a signal light,—
One, if by land, and two, if by sea;
And I on the opposite shore will be,
Ready to ride and spread the alarm
Through every Middlesex village and farm,
For the country-folk to be up and to arm."

3
Then he said, "Good-night!" and with muffled oar
Silently rowed to the Charlestown shore,
Just as the moon rose over the bay,
Where swinging wide at her moorings lay
The *Somerset*, British man-of-war;
A phantom ship, with each mast and spar
Across the moon like a prison bar,
And a huge black hulk, that was magnified
By its own reflection in the tide.

4
Meanwhile, his friend, through alley and street,
Wanders and watches with eager ears,
Till in the silence around him he hears

The muster of men at the barrack door,
The sound of arms, and the tramp of feet,
And the measured tread of the grenadiers,
Marching down to their boats on the shore.

5

Then he climbed to the tower of the church,
Up the wooden stairs, with stealthy tread,
To the belfry-chamber overhead,
And startled the pigeons from their perch
On the sombre rafters, that round him made
Masses and moving shapes of shade—
Up the trembling ladder, steep and tall,
To the highest window in the wall,
Where he paused to listen and look down
A moment on the roofs of the town,
And the moonlight flowing over all.

6

Beneath, in the churchyard lay the dead,
In their night-encampment on the hill,
Wrapped in silence so deep and still
That he could hear, like a sentinel's tread,
The watchful night-wind, as it went
Creeping along from tent to tent,
And seeming to whisper, "All is well!"
A moment only he feels the spell
Of the place and the hour, and the secret dread
Of the lonely belfry and the dead;
For suddenly all his thoughts are bent
On a shadowy something far away,
Where the river widens to meet the bay—
A line of black that bends and floats
On the rising tide, like a bridge of boats.

7
Meanwhile, impatient to mount and ride,
Booted and spurred, with a heavy stride
On the opposite shore walked Paul Revere.
Now he patted his horse's side,
Now gazed at the landscape far and near,
Then, impetuous, stamped the earth
And turned and tightened his saddle-girth;
But most he watched with eager search
The belfry tower of the Old North Church,
As it rose above the graves on the hill,
Lonely and spectral and sombre and still.
And lo! as he looks, on the belfry's height
A glimmer, and then a gleam of light!
He springs to the saddle, the bridle he turns,
But lingers and gazes, till full on his sight
A second lamp in the belfry burns!

8
A hurry of hoofs in a village street,
A shape in the moonlight, a bulk in the dark,
And beneath from the pebbles, in passing, a spark
Struck out by a steed flying fearless and fleet;

That was all! And yet, through the gloom and the light,
The fate of a nation was riding that night;
And the spark struck out by that steed, in his flight,
Kindled the land into flame with its heat.

9

He has left the village and mounted the steep,
And beneath him, tranquil and broad and deep,
Is the Mystic, meeting the ocean tides;
And under the alders that skirt its edge,
Now soft on the sand, now loud on the ledge,
Is heard the tramp of his steed as he rides.

10

It was twelve by the village clock
When he crossed the bridge into Medford town.
He heard the crowing of the cock,
And the barking of the farmer's dog,
And felt the damp of the river fog,
That rises after the sun goes down.

11

It was one by the village clock
When he galloped into Lexington.
He saw the gilded weathercock
Swim in the moonlight as he passed,
And the meeting-house windows, blank and bare,
Gaze at him with a spectral glare,
As if they already stood aghast
At the bloody work they would look upon.

12

It was two by the village clock
When he came to the bridge in Concord town.

He heard the bleating of the flock,
And the twitter of birds among the trees,
And felt the breath of the morning breeze
Blowing over the meadows brown.
And one was safe and asleep in his bed
Who at the bridge would be first to fall,
Who that day would be lying dead,
Pierced by a British musket-ball.

13
You know the rest. In the books you have read
How the British Regulars fired and fled—
How the farmers gave them ball for ball,
From behind each fence and farmyard wall,
Chasing the Red-coats down the lane,
Then crossing the fields to emerge again
Under the trees at the turn of the road,
And only pausing to fire and load.

14
So through the night rode Paul Revere;
And so through the night went his cry of alarm
To every Middlesex village and farm,
A cry of defiance and not of fear,
A voice in the darkness, a knock at the door,
And a word that shall echo for evermore!
For, borne on the night-wind of the Past,
Through all our history, to the last,
In the hour of darkness and peril and need,
The people will waken and listen to hear
The hurrying hoof-beats of that steed,
And the midnight message of Paul Revere.

H. W. Longfellow

ANNABEL LEE

It was many and many a year ago,
    In a kingdom by the sea,
That a maiden there lived whom you may know
    By the name of Annabel Lee;
And this maiden she lived with no other thought
Than to love and be loved by me.

She was a child and I was a child,
    In this kingdom by the sea,
But we loved with a love that was more than love—
    I and my Annabel Lee—
With a love that the winged seraphs of Heaven
    Coveted her and me.

And this was the reason that, long ago,
    In this kingdom by the sea,
A wind blew out of a cloud by night
    Chilling my Annabel Lee;
So that her highborn kinsmen came
    And bore her away from me,
To shut her up in a sepulchre
    In this kingdom by the sea.

The angels, not half so happy in Heaven,
    Went envying her and me:
Yes! that was the reason (as all men know,
    In this kingdom by the sea)
That the wind came out of the cloud, chilling
    And killing my Annabel Lee.

But our love it was stronger by far than the love
    Of those who were older than we—
    Of many far wiser than we—
And neither the angels in heaven above
    Nor the demons down under the sea,
Can ever dissever my soul from the soul
    Of the beautiful Annabel Lee—

For the moon never beams without bringing me dreams
    Of the beautiful Annabel Lee;
And the stars never rise but I see the bright eyes
    Of the beautiful Annabel Lee;
And so, all the night-tide, I lie down by the side
Of my darling, my darling, my life and my bride,
    In her sepulchre there by the sea—
    In her tomb by the sounding sea.

Edgar Allan Poe

THE EMPEROR AMD THE BIRD'S NEST

Once the Emperor, Charles of Spain,
   With his swarthy, grave commanders,
I forget in what campaign,
Long besieged, in mud and rain,
   Some old frontier town of Flanders.

Up and down the dreary camp,
   In great boots of Spanish leather,
Striding with a measured tramp,
These Hidalgos, dull and damp,
   Cursed the Frenchmen, cursed the weather.

Thus as to and fro they went
   Over upland and through hollow,
Giving their impatience vent,
Perched upon the Emperor's tent,
   In her nest, they spied a swallow.

Yes, it was a swallow's nest,
  Built of clay and hair of horses,
Mane, or tail, or dragoon's crest,
Found on hedgerows east and west,
  After skirmish of the forces.

Then an old Hidalgo said,
  As he twirled his grey mustachio,
"Sure this swallow overhead
Thinks the Emperor's tent a shed,
  And the Emperor's but a Macho!"

Hearing his imperial name
  Coupled with those words of malice,
Half in anger, half in shame,
Forth the great campaigner came
  Slowly from his canvas palace.

"Let no hand the bird molest,"
  Said he solemnly, "nor hurt her!"
Adding then, by way of jest,
"Golondrina is my guest,
  'Tis the wife of some deserter!"

Swift as bowstring speeds a shaft,
  Through the camp was spread the rumour,
And the soldiers as they quaffed
Flemish beer at dinner, laughed
  At the Emperor's pleasant humour.

So unharmed and unafraid
  Sat the swallow still and brooded.
Till the constant cannonade
Through the walls a breach had made,

And the siege was thus concluded.
Then the army, elsewhere bent,
    Struck its tents as if disbanding,
Only not the Emperor's tent,
For he ordered, ere he went,
    Very curtly, "Leave it standing."

So it stood there all alone,
    Loosely flapping, torn and shattered,
Till the brood was fledged and flown,
Singing o'er those walls of stone
    Which the cannon-shot had shattered.

H. W. Longfellow

WHEN THE PLANE DIVED

When the plane dived and the machine-gun spattered
The deck, in his numb clutch the tugging wheel
Bucked madly as he strove to keep the keel
Zig-zagging through the steep and choppy sea—
To keep zig-zagging, that was all that mattered—
To keep the ship zig-zagging endlessly,
Dodging that diving devil. Now again,
The bullets spattered like a squall of rain
About him; and again with desperate grip
He tugged, to port the helm . . . to keep the ship
Zig-zagging . . . zagging through eternity;
To keep the ship . . . A sudden scalding pain
Shot through his shoulder and the whole sky shattered
About him in red fire; and yet his grip
Tightened upon the wheel. . . To keep the ship
Zig . . . zig . . . zig-zagging, that was all that mattered.

Wilfrid Gibson

THE KITE

It was a day
All blue and lifting white,
When I went into the fields with
Frank
To fly his kite.

The fields were aged, bare,
Shut between houses everywhere.
All the way there
The wind tugged at the kite to take it
Untethered, toss and break it;
But Frank held fast, and I
Walked with him admiringly;
In his light brave and fine
How bright was mine!

We tailed the kite
While the wind flapped its purple
face
And yellow head.
Frank's yellow head
Was scarcely higher, and not so
bright.
"Let go!" he cried, and I let go
And watched the kite
Swaying and rising so
That I was rooted to the place,
Watching the kite
Rise into the blue,

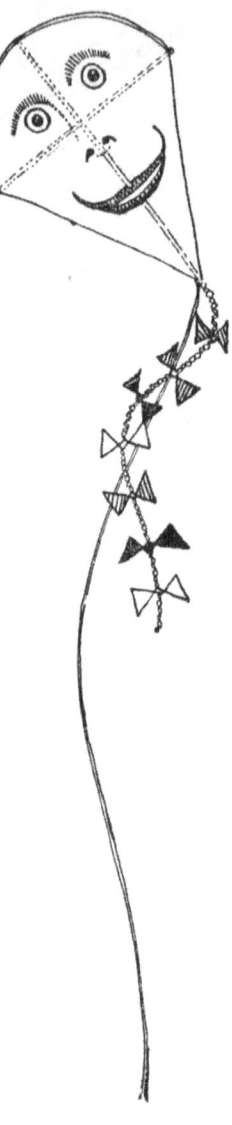

Lifting its head against the white,
Against the sun,
Against the height
That far off, farther drew;
Shivering there
In that fine air

As we below shivered with delight
And fear.

There it floated
Among the birds and clouds at ease
Of others all unnoted,
Swimming above the ranked stiff trees.
And I lay down, looking up at the sky,
The clouds and birds that floated
By others still unnoted,
And that swaying kite
Specking the light:
Looking up at the sky
The birds and clouds that drew
Nearer, leaving the blue,
Stooping, and then brushing me,
With such tenderness touching me
That I had still lain there
In those fields bare,
Forgetting the kite;
For every cloud was now a kite
Streaming with light.

John Freeman

THE SAILOR'S CONSOLATION

One night came on a hurricane,
The sea was mountains rolling,
When Barney Buntline slewed his quid,
And said to Billy Bowline:
"A strong nor-wester's blowing, Bill,
Hark! don't ye hear it roar now!
Lord help 'em, how I pities them
Unhappy folks on shore now.

"Foolhardy chaps as live in towns,
What danger they are all in,
And now lie quaking in their beds,
For fear the roof should fall in!

"Poor creatures, how they envies us,
And wishes, I've a notion,
For our good luck in such a storm,
To be upon the ocean!

"And as for them that's out all day,
On business from their houses,
And late at night returning home,
To cheer their babes and spouses;
While you and I, Bill, on the deck
Are comfortable lying,
My eyes! what tiles and chimney-pots
About their heads are flying!

"Both you and I have oft-times heard
How men are killed and undone,
By overturns from carriages,
By thieves, and fires in London,

We know what risks these landsmen run,
From noblemen to tailors;
Then, Bill, let us thank Providence
That you and I are sailors."

Charles Dibdin

THE BEGGAR MAID

Her arms across her breast she laid;
    She was more fair than words can say:
Bare-footed came the beggar maid
    Before the king Cophetua.
In robe and crown the king stept down,
    To meet and greet her on her way:
"It is no wonder," said the lords,
    "She is more beautiful than day."

As shines the moon in clouded skies,
    She in her poor attire was seen:
One praised her ankles, one her eyes,
    One her dark hair and lovesome mien.
So sweet a face, such angel grace,
    In all that land had never been:
Cophetua sware a royal oath:
    "This beggar maid shall be my queen!"

Alfred, Lord Tennyson

THE THREE FISHERS

Three fishers went sailing away to the West,
    Away to the West as the sun went down;
Each thought on the woman who loved him the best,
    And the children stood watching them out of the town;
For men must work and women must weep,
And there's little to earn, and many to keep,
    Though the harbour bar be moaning.

Three wives sat up in the lighthouse tower,
    And they trimmed the lamps as the sun went down;
They looked at the squall, and they looked at the shower,
    And the night-rack came rolling up ragged and brown.
But men must work and women must weep,
Though storms be sudden, and waters deep,
    And the harbour bar be moaning.

Three corpses lay out on the shining sands
    In the morning gleam as the tide went down,
And the women are weeping and wringing their hands
    For those who will never come home to the town:
For men must work and women must weep,
And the sooner it's over, the sooner to sleep;
    And good-bye to the bar and its moaning.
Charles Kingsley

THE GOOSE

I knew an old wife lean and poor,
    Her rags scarce held together;
There strode a stranger to the door,
    And it was windy weather.

He held a goose upon his arm,
    He uttered rhyme and reason,
"Here, take the goose, and keep you warm,
    It is a stormy season."

She caught the white goose by the leg,
    A goose—'twas no great matter.
The goose let fall a golden egg
    With cackle and with clatter.

She dropped the goose, and caught the pelf,
    And ran to tell her neighbours;
And blessed herself, and cursed herself,
    And rested from her labours.

And feeding high, and living soft,
    Grew plump and able-bodied;
Until the grave churchwarden doffed,
    The parson smirked and nodded.

So sitting, served by man and maid,
    She felt her heart grow prouder:
But ah! the more the white goose laid
    It clacked and cackled louder.

It cluttered here, it chuckled there
    It stirred the old wife's mettle:
She shifted in her elbow-chair,
    And hurled the pan and kettle.

"A quinsy choke thy cursed note!"
    Then waxed her anger stronger.
"Go, take the goose, and wring her throat,
    I will not bear it longer."

Then yelped the cur, and yawled the cat;
    Ran Gaffer, stumbled Gammer.
The goose flew this way and flew that,
    And filled the house with clamour.

As head and heels upon the floor
    They floundered all together,
There strode a stranger to the door,
    And it was windy weather:

He took the goose upon his arm,
    He uttered words of scorning;
"So keep you cold, or keep you warm,
    It is a stormy morning."

The wild wind rang from park and plain,
    And round the attics rumbled,
Till all the tables danced again,
    And half the chimneys tumbled.

The glass blew in, the fire blew out,
    The blast was hard and harder.
Her cap blew off, her gown blew up,
    And a whirlwind cleared the larder;

And while on all sides breaking loose
    Her household fled the danger,
Quoth she, "The Devil take the goose,
    And God forget the stranger!"

Alfred, Lord Tennyson

THE OLD NAVY

The captain stood on the carronade: "First lieutenant," says he,
"Send all my merry men aft here, for they must list to me;
I haven't the gift of the gab, my sons—because I'm bred to the sea;
That ship there is a Frenchman, who means to fight with we.
And odds, bobs, hammer and tongs—but I've gained the victory!

"That ship there is a Frenchman, and if we don't take *she*,
Tis a thousand bullets to one, that she will capture *we*;
I haven't the gift of the gab, my boys; so each man to his gun;
If she's not mine in half-an-hour, I'll flog each mother's son.
For odds, bobs, hammer and tongs, long as I've been to sea,
I've fought 'gainst every odds—and I've gained the victory!"

We fought for twenty minutes, when the Frenchman had enough;
"I little thought," said he, "that your men were of such stuff";

Our captain took the Frenchman's sword, a low bow made to
   he;
"I haven't the gift of the gab, mounseer, but polite I wish to be.
And odds bobs, hammer and tongs, long as I've been to sea,
I've fought 'gainst every odds—and I've gained the victory!"

Our captain sent for all of us: "My merry men," said he,
"I haven't the gift of the gab, my lads, but yet I thankful be;
You've done your duty handsomely, each man stood to his
   gun;
If you hadn't, you villains, as sure as day, I'd have flogged each
   mother's son,
For odds bobs, hammer and tongs, as long as I'm at sea,
I'll fight 'gainst every odds—and I'll gain the victory!"

Captain Marryat

PELTERS OF PYRAMIDS

A shoal of idlers, from a merchant craft
Anchor'd off Alexandria, went ashore,
And mounting asses in their headlong glee,
Round Pompey's Pillar rode with hoots and taunts,
As men oft say, "What art thou more than we?"
Next in a boat they floated up the Nile,
Singing and drinking, swearing senseless oaths,
Shouting, and laughing most derisively
At all majestic scenes. A bank they reach'd,
And clambering up, play'd gambols among tombs;
And in portentous ruins (through whose depths,
The mighty twilight of departed Gods,
Both sun and moon glanced furtive, as in awe)
They hid, and whoop'd, and spat on sacred things.

At length, beneath the blazing sun they lounged
Near a great Pyramid. Awhile they stood
With stupid stare, until resentment grew,
In the recoil of meanness from the vast;
And gathering stones, they with coarse oaths and jibes
(As they would say, "What art thou more than we?")
Pelted the Pyramid! But soon these men,
Hot and exhausted, sat them down to drink—
Wrangled, smok'd, spat, and laugh'd, and drowsily
Curs'd the bald Pyramid and fell asleep.

Night came: a little sand went drifting by—
And morn again was in the soft blue heavens.
The broad slopes of the shining Pyramid
Look'd down in their austere simplicity
Upon the glistening silence of the sands
Whereon no trace of mortal dust was seen.

Richard Hengist Horne

THE DESTINED HOUR

To Abou Seyd his servant came, Hussein,
With ashen lips—"O Master, let me go
Home to Samarra—I would come again
    In three days' space."
Then, with a smile upon his sword-scarred face,
The old Seyd answered: "Son, what drives thee so?
Some sudden trouble? Nay, I need not know.
For Allah is the Lord of all men's ways."

"O Master, listen—I will tell thee why.
In our bazaar but now I saw there stood
A stranger, tall and silent. Passing by,
I peered into his face. But ah, my breath
    Failed. For beneath his hood
Two eyes burned-hollow. Master it was Death!
He raised his hand to strike. Oh let me fly!—
Though Allah is the Lord of all men's days."

Then Abou Seyd, old captain that had seen
A hundred times across the battle glide
The face of Death, inclined his head, serene;
And Hussein vanished through the columned court.
    But laying God's word aside,
Across the noonday glare his Master sought
The buzz of the bazaar. "Poor fool!" he thought.
Yet Allah is the Lord of all men's ways."

Loud swarmed the buyers round each booth and stall;
But there by Omar's Mosque, at the market's end,
Watched one shape like a shadow, gaunt and tall.
Then, drawing near, said Abou Seyd, "My friend,
Why threaten my poor slave—so wantonly—

That harmed thee not at all?
In my hot youth I might have threatened thee,
Forgetting Allah, Lord of all men's days."

Then that dark face upon him bent such eyes,
The scar upon Seyd's cheek grew grey with fear.
"I threatened not thy servant, Abou Seyd.
   But in surprise
I raised my hand, to see him standing near.
For this same night God bids my hand be laid
Upon him at Samarra, far from here.
Yet Allah is the Lord of all men's ways."

F. L. Lucas

THE VISION OF BELSHAZZAR

The King was on his throne,
The Satraps thronged the hall:
A thousand bright lamps shone
O'er that bright festival.
A thousand cups of gold,
In Judah deem'd divine—
Jehovah's vessels hold
The godless heathen's wine.

In that same hour and hall,
The fingers of a hand
Came forth against the wall
And wrote as if on sand:
The fingers of a man:
A solitary hand
Along the letters ran,

And traced them like a wand.

The monarch saw, and shook,
And bade no more rejoice;
All bloodless wax'd his look,
And tremulous his voice.
"Let the men of lore appear,
The wisest of the earth,
And expound the words of fear
Which mar our royal mirth."

Chaldea's seers are good,
But here they have no skill:
And the unknown letters stood
Untold and aweful still.
And Babel's men of age
Are wise and deep in lore;
But now they were not sage,
They saw—but knew no more.

A captive in the land,
A stranger and a youth,
He heard the king's command,
He saw that writing's truth.
The lamps around were bright,
The prophecy in view;
He read it on that night,—
The morrow proved it true.

"Belshazzar's grave is made,
His kingdom passed away,
He, in the balance weigh'd,
Is light and worthless clay;

The shroud his robe of state,
His canopy the stone;
The Mede is at the gate!
The Persian on his throne."

Lord Byron

THE COLUBRIAD

Close by the threshold of a door nail'd fast
Three kittens sat: each kitten look'd aghast.
I, passing swift and inattentive by,
At the three kittens cast a careless eye;
Not much concerned to know what they did there,
Not deeming kittens worth a poet's care.
But presently a loud and furious hiss
Caused me to stop, and to exclaim—what's this?
When, lo! upon the threshold met my view,
With head erect, and eyes of fiery hue,
A viper, long as Count de Grasse's queue.
Forth from his head his forked tongue he throws,
Darting it full against a kitten's nose;
Who having never seen in field or house
The like, sat still and silent, as a mouse:
Only, projecting with attention due
Her whiskered face, she ask'd him—who are you?
On to the hall went I, with pace not slow,
But swift as lightning, for a long Dutch hoe;
With which well arm'd I hastened to the spot
To find the viper. But I found him not,
And, turning up the leaves and shrubs around,
Found only, that he was not to be found.
But still the kittens, sitting as before,

Sat watching close the bottom of the door.

I hope—said I—the villain I would kill
Has slipt between the door and the window sill;
And if I make despatch, and follow hard,
No doubt but I shall find him in the yard;
For long ere now it should have been rehearsed
'Twas in the garden that I found him first.
E'en there I found him; there the full-grown cat
His head with velvet paw did gently pat,
As curious as the kittens erst had been
To learn what this phenomenon might mean.
Fill'd with heroic ardour at the sight,
And fearing every moment he would bite,
And rob our household of our only cat
That was of age to combat with a rat,
With out-stretch'd hoe I slew him at the door,
And taught him *never to come there no more.*

William Cowper

NIGHT WITH A WOLF

High up on the lonely mountains,
    Where the wild men watched and waited:
Wolves in the forest, and bears in the bush,
    And I on my path belated.

The rain and the night together
    Came down, and the wind came after,
Bending the props of the pine-tree roof,
    And snapping many a rafter.

I crept along in the darkness,
    Stunned and bruised, and blinded—
Crept to a fir with thick-set boughs,
    And a sheltering rock behind it.

There, from the blowing and raining
    Crouching, I sought to hide me:
Something rustled, two green eyes shone,
    And a wolf lay down beside me.

Listener, be not frightened;
    I and the wolf together,
Side by side, through the long, long night,
    Hid from the awful weather.

His wet fur pressed against me;
    Each of us warmed the other:
Each of us felt, in the stormy dark,
    That beast and man was brother.

And when the falling forest
   No longer crashed in warning,
Each of us went from our hiding-place
   Forth in the wild, wet morning.

J. B. Taylor

ELEGY ON THE DEATH OF A MAD DOG

Good people all, of every sort,
   Give ear unto my song;
And if you find it wondrous short,
   It cannot hold you long.

In Islington there was a man,
   Of whom the world might say,
That still a godly race he ran,
   Whene'er he went to pray.

A kind and gentle heart he had,
   To comfort friends and foes;
The naked every day he clad,
   When he put on his clothes.

And in that town a dog was found,
    As many dogs there be,
Both mongrel, puppy, whelp, and hound,
    And curs of low degree.

This dog and man at first were friends;
    But when a pique began,
The dog, to gain some private ends,
    Went mad and bit the man.

Around from all the neighbouring streets,
    The wond'ring neighbours ran,
And swore the dog had lost its wits,
    To bite so good a man.

The wound it seem'd both sore and sad
    To every Christian eye;
And while they swore the dog was mad,
    They swore the man would die.

But soon a wonder came to light,
    That showed the rogues they lied:
The man recovered of the bite,
    The dog it was that died.

Oliver Goldsmith

THE REBEL SOLDIER

One morning, one morning, one morning in May,
I heard a poor soldier lamenting and say,
I heard a poor soldier lamenting and mourn:
I am a rebel soldier and far from my home.

It's grape-shot and musket and the cannons lumber loud.
There's many a mangled body, a blanket for their shroud,
There's many a mangled body left on the field alone.
I am a rebel soldier and far from my home.

I'll eat when I'm hungry and drink when I'm dry.
If the Yankees don't kill me I'll live until I die,
If the Yankees don't kill me and cause me to mourn.
I am a rebel soldier and far from my home.

I'll build me a castle on some green mountain high,
Where the wild geese can see me as they do pass me by,
Where the wild geese can see me and hear my sad mourn:
I am a rebel soldier and far from my home.

American Folk Song

SHAMEFUL DEATH

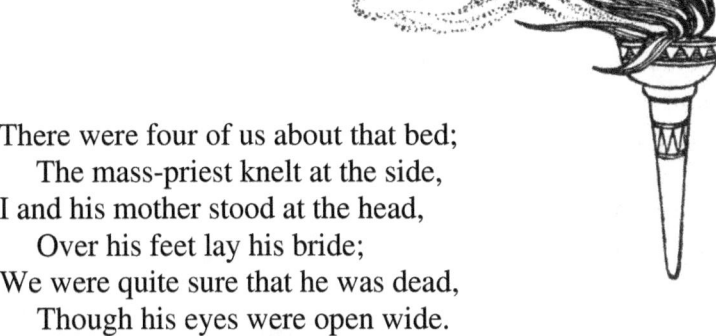

There were four of us about that bed;
    The mass-priest knelt at the side,
I and his mother stood at the head,
    Over his feet lay his bride;
We were quite sure that he was dead,
    Though his eyes were open wide.

He did not die in the night,
    He did not die in the day,
But in the morning twilight
    His spirit passed away,
When neither sun nor moon was bright,
    And the trees were merely grey.

He was not slain with the sword,
    Knight's axe, or the knightly spear,
Yet spoke he never a word
    After he came in here;
I cut away the cord
    From the neck of my brother dear.

He did not strike one blow,
    For the recreants came behind,
In a place where the hornbeams grow,
    A path right hard to find,
For the hornbeam boughs swing so,
    That the twilight makes it blind.

They lighted a great torch then,
    When his arms were pinioned fast.
Sir John the knight of the Fen,
    Sir Guy of the Dolorous Blast,
With knights threescore and ten,
    Hung brave Lord Hugh at last.

I am threescore and ten,
    And my hair is turned all grey,
But I met Sir John of the Fen
Long ago on a summer day,
And am glad to think of the moment when
I took his life away.

I am threescore and ten,
    And my strength is mostly passed,
    But long ago I and my men,
When the sky was overcast,
And the smoke rolled over the reeds of the fen,
    Slew Guy of the Dolorous Blast.

And now, knights all of you,
    I pray you pray for Sir Hugh,
A good knight and a true,
    And for Alice, his wife, pray too.

William Morris

FROM *HORATIUS*

1
Lars Porsena of Clusium
    By the Nine Gods he swore
That the great house of Tarquin
    Should suffer wrong no more.
By the Nine Gods he swore it,
    And named a trysting day,
And bade his messengers ride forth,
East and west and south and north,
    To summon his array.

2
Fast by the royal standard,
    O'erlooking all the war,
Lars Porsena of Clusium
    Sat in his ivory car.
By the right wheel rode Mamilius,
    Prince of the Latian name;
And by the left false Sextus,
    That wrought the deed of shame.

3
But when the face of Sextus
    Was seen among the foes,
A yell that rent the firmament
    From all the town arose.
On the house-tops was no woman
    But spat towards him and hissed,
No child but screamed out curses,
    And shook its little fist.

4
But the Consul's brow was sad,
    And the Consul's speech was low
And darkly looked he at the wall
    And darkly at the foe:
"Their van will be upon us
    Before the bridge goes down;
And if they once may win the bridge,
    What hope to save the town?"

5
Then out spake brave Horatius,
    The Captain of the Gate:
"To every man upon this earth
    Death cometh soon or late.
And how can man die better
    Than facing fearful odds
For the ashes of his fathers
    And the temples of his Gods.

6
"And for the tender mother
    Who dandled him to rest,
And for the wife who nurses

    His baby at her breast,
And for the holy maidens
    Who feed the eternal flame—
To save them from false Sextus
    That wrought the deed of shame?

7

"Hew down the bridge, Sir Consul,
    With all the speed ye may;
I, with two more to help me,
    Will hold the foe in play.
In yon strait path a thousand
    May well be stopped by three:
Now who will stand on either hand
    And keep the bridge with me?"

8

Then out spake Spurius Lartius—
    A Ramnian proud was he:
"Lo, I will stand at thy right hand,
    And keep the bridge with thee."
And out spake strong Herminius—
    Of Titian blood was he:
"I will abide on thy left side,
    And keep the bridge with thee."

9

"Horatius," quoth the Consul,
    "As thou sayest so let it be."
And straight against that great array
    Forth went the dauntless Three.
For Romans in Rome's quarrel
    Spared neither land nor gold,

Nor son, nor wife, nor limb, nor life,
    In the brave days of old.

10
Then none was for a party;
    Then all were for the state;
Then the great man helped the poor,
    And the poor man loved the great:
Then lands were fairly portioned;
    Then spoils were fairly sold:
The Romans were like brothers
    In the brave days of old.

11
Now Roman is to Roman
    More hateful than a foe,
And the Tribunes beard the high,
    And the fathers grind the low.
As we wax hot in faction,
    In battle we wax cold;
Wherefore men fight not as they fought
    In the brave days of old.

12
Was none who would be foremost
    To lead such dire attack;
But those behind cried "Forward!"
    And those before cried, "Back!"
And backward now and forward
    Wavers the deep array;
And on the tossing sea of steel
    To and fro the standards reel
And the victorious trumpet-peal
    Dies fitfully away.

13
Yet one man for one moment
    Stood out before the crowd;
Well known was he to all the Three,
    And they gave him greeting loud:
"Now welcome, welcome, Sextus!
    Now welcome to thy home!
Why dost thou stay, and turn away?
    Here lies the road to Rome."

14
Thrice looked he at the city;
    Thrice looked he at the dead;
And thrice came on in fury,
    And thrice turned back in dread;
And, white with fear and hatred,
    Scowled at the narrow way
Where, wallowing in a pool of blood,
    The bravest Tuscans lay.

15
But meanwhile axe and lever
    Have manfully been plied;
And now the bridge hangs tottering
    Above the boiling tide.
"Come back, come back, Horatius!"

Loud cried the Fathers all—
"Back, Lartius! back, Herminius!
  Back, ere the ruin fall!"

16
Back darted Spurius Lartius—
  Herminius darted back;
And, as they passed, beneath their feet
  They felt the timbers crack.
But when they turned their faces,
  And on the farther shore
Saw brave Horatius stand alone,
  They would have crossed once more;

17
But with a crash like thunder
  Fell every loosened beam,
And, like a dam, the mighty wreck
  Lay right athwart the stream:
And a long shout of triumph
Rose from the walls of Rome,
As to the highest turret-tops
Was splashed the yellow foam.

18
And, like a horse unbroken,
  When first he feels the rein,
The furious river struggles hard,
  And tossed his tawny mane,
And burst the curb, and bounded,
  Rejoicing to be free;
And whirling down, in fierce career,
Battlement, and plank, and pier,
  Rushed headlong to the sea.

19
Alone stood brave Horatius,
But constant still in mind—
Thrice thirty thousand foes before,
And the broad flood behind.
"Down with him!" cried false Sextus,
With a smile on his pale face;
"Now yield thee," cried Lars Porsena,
"Now yield thee to our grace."

20
Round turned he, as not deigning
    Those craven ranks to see;
Naught spake he to Lars Porsena,
    To Sextus naught spake he;
But he saw on Palatinus
    The white porch of his home;
And he spake to the noble river
That rolls by the towers of Rome:

21
"O Tiber! Father Tiber!
    To whom the Romans pray,
A Roman's life, a Roman's arms,
    Take thou in charge this day!"
So he spake, and speaking, sheathed
    The good sword by his side,
And, with his harness on his back,
    Plunged headlong in the tide.

22
No sound of joy or sorrow
    Was heard from either bank,
But friends and foes in dumb surprise,
With parted lips and straining eyes,
    Stood gazing where he sank;
And when above the surges
    They saw his crest appear,
All Rome sent forth a rapturous cry,
And even the ranks of Tuscany
    Could scarce forbear to cheer.

23
But fiercely ran the current,
    Swollen high by months of rain;
And fast his blood was flowing,
    And he was sore in pain,
And heavy with his armour,
    And spent with clanging blows;
And oft they thought him sinking,
    But still again he rose.

24
Never, I ween, did swimmer,
    In such an evil case,
Struggle through such a raging flood
    Safe to the landing-place;
But his limbs were borne up bravely
    By the brave heart within,
And our good Father Tiber
    Bore bravely up his chin.

25
"Curse on him!" quoth false Sextus—
    "Will not the villain drown?
But for this stay, ere close of day
    We should have sacked the town!"
"Heaven help him!" quoth Lars Porsena,
    "And bring him safe to shore;
For such a gallant feat of arms
    Was never seen before."

26
And now he feels the bottom;
    Now on dry earth he stands;
Now round him throng the Fathers
    To press his gory hands;
And now, with shouts and clapping,
    And noise of weeping loud,
He enters through the River-Gate,
    Borne by the joyous crowd.

27
When the oldest cask is opened,
    And the largest lamp is lit;
When the chestnuts glow in the embers,
    And the kid turns on the spit;
When young and old in circle
    Around the firebrands close;
When the girls are weaving baskets,
    And the lads are shaping bows;

28
When the goodman mends his armour,
    And trims his helmet plume;
When the goodwife's shuttle merrily
    Goes flashing through the loom;
With weeping and with laughter
    Still is the story told,
How well Horatius kept the bridge
    In the brave days of old.

Lord Macaulay

A MARRIAGE RING

The ring, so worn as you behold,
So thin, so pale, is yet of gold:
The passion such it was to prove—
Worn with life's care, love yet was love.

George Crabbe

ABOU BEN ADHEM

Abou Ben Adhem (may his tribe increase!)
Awoke one night from a deep dream of peace,
And saw, within the moonlight in his room,
Making it rich, and like a lily in bloom,
An angel writing in a book of gold:
Exceeding peace had made Ben Adhem bold,
And to the presence in the room he said,
"What writest thou?"—The vision raised its head,
And with a look made of all sweet accord,
Answer'd, "The names of those that love the Lord."
"And is mine one?" said Abou. "Nay, not so,"
Replied the angel. Abou spoke more low,
But cheerly still; and said, "I pray thee, then,
Write me as one that loves his fellow men."
The angel wrote and vanish'd. The next night
It came again with a great wakening light,
And show'd the names whom love of God had blest,
And lo! Ben Adhem's name led all the rest.

Leigh Hunt

THE CHARGE OF THE LIGHT BRIGADE

Half a league, half a league,
Half a league onward,
All in the valley of Death,
    Rode the six hundred.
"Forward the Light Brigade!
Charge for the guns!" he said:
Into the valley of Death
    Rode the six hundred.

"Forward the Light Brigade!"
Was there a man dismay'd?
Not tho' the soldier knew
    Some one had blunder'd:
Theirs not to make reply,
Theirs not to reason why,
Theirs but to do and die:
Into the valley of Death
    Rode the six hundred.

Cannon to right of them,
Cannon to left of them,
Cannon in front of them
    Volley'd and thunder'd;

Storm'd at with shot and shell,
Boldly they rode and well,
Into the jaws of Death,
Into the mouth of Hell
   Rode the six hundred.

Flash'd all their sabres bare,
Flash'd as they turn'd in air,
Sabring the gunners there,
Charging an army, while
   All the world wonder'd:
Plunged in the battery-smoke
Right thro' the line they broke;
Cossack and Russian
Reel'd from the sabre-stroke
Shatter'd and sunder'd.
Then they rode back, but not,
   Not the six hundred.

Cannon to right of them,
Cannon to left of them,
Cannon behind them
   Volley'd and thunder'd;
Storm'd at with shot and shell,
While horse and hero fell,

They that had fought so well
Came thro' the jaws of Death
Back from the mouth of Hell
All that was left of them,
   Left of six hundred.

When can their glory fade?
O the wild charge they made!
   All the world wonder'd.
Honour the charge they made!
Honour the Light Brigade,
   Noble six hundred!

Alfred, Lord Tennyson

INTRODUCTION TO THE TEACHING AND LEARNING NOTES AND GUIDE
BOOK FOUR

Part One of Book Four of *Poems to Enjoy* contains poems suitable for reading aloud. Part Two consists of a selection of descriptive poetry and Part Three provides a number of narrative poems.

A variety of material is thus provided for a variety of teaching methods. Sometimes the students can simply listen as the teacher reads aloud or plays from the audio recording a number of poems, perhaps with a related, or similar theme. At other times the students may take part in the reading themselves, either individually, or in groups. When a poem is suitable, it can be discussed after the teacher has read it aloud and/or after the audio recording has been played. If it is vividly descriptive, the students can often be encouraged to sketch or paint from their imagination.

Whatever the approach, poetry can mean a great deal to Secondary School students at this stage. They should now be better equipped to understand more completely the purpose, thoughts and moods of the poet. Taste is beginning to develop and the student is starting to discriminate. The teacher can assist this development, if he introduces an interesting diversity of poetic material and if he avoids the assumption that the students ought to like certain poems, even if they do not.

The following observations are amplified in the Teaching Notes, as they apply to individual poems:

1. Poems to Speak

The poems most suitable for reading aloud, whether individually, in chorus, or in groups, are those which have a pronounced rhythmic and musical quality. The choice of material is particularly important and it should be borne in mind that only certain poems are suitable for choral reading. The teacher should avoid (a) poems which are too personal in quality—e.g. many lyrics, (b) long narrative poems and (c) extensive descriptive passages, unrelieved by dialogue of any kind. Whether a poem should be spoken by the class as a whole in unison, or whether it should be said by individuals, or by groups of 'dark' or 'light' voices, depends upon the teacher and, even better, upon the agreement of students and teacher after discussion. Every poem which is at all suitable for choral work is open to much variation and the suggestions in the Notes should not therefore be taken as always applicable.

The teacher should not force a particular way of delivering the poem on the students. The teacher should refrain, if possible, from interrupting the readings to make corrections of pronunciation and inflection.

2. Pictures in Poetry

Part Two in Book Four contains a number of poems which, because of their vivid pictorial quality, should increase the students' ability to visualise, in one form or another, what has been described. In most cases, students are likely to 'see' better when they have been able to listen to a good reading by the teacher and/or the audio-recording attached to this book. At this point, it is worthwhile emphasizing the importance of the teacher's role as poetry reader. Many a well-planned lesson has failed because of the teacher's inability to present a poem with the sensitivity it deserves. Two or three poems can often be read to create the right atmosphere for a lesson in which the aim is to encourage the students to sketch or paint from the imagination. Once this atmosphere has been achieved, the creative work can begin. Illustrations of a high standard should not be expected and the tendency should always be to praise, rather than to condemn, especially when it is obvious that there has been some effort. No piece of original work should be given any kind of numerical mark, or, indeed, "marked" at all.

3. The Poet as Storyteller

A majority of the poems to be found in Part Three of Book Four should provide good material for discussion and a skilful teacher should also be able to use some of them as examples before a lesson devoted to the students' own original writing. The success of the poetry-writing lesson will depend primarily upon the atmosphere which the teacher has succeeded in creating and maintaining. S/he should, for example, do everything s/he can to prevent untimely interruptions from outside the room. S/he might read some poems to the class himself at the beginning of the lesson, or play some from the audio of the text, to put the students into the right frame of mind. S/he should be ready to give advice freely, whilst, at the same time, remaining patient with work, which may, perhaps, be rather crude. Lessons of this type, if they are arranged regularly, will almost certainly help to improve both written and spoken English and the teacher will be able to see how concentration on the creative approach to poetry has increased the students' interest in it.

The amount of discussion which will follow the teacher's readings will vary according to the interest and ability of the class and according to the poems that have been read. Although in many instances questions have been suggested in the Teaching and Learning Notes and Guide, a teacher who wishes to maintain interest will avoid the dissection and explanation of every line, unless he feels this to be vitally necessary.

TEACHING AND LEARNING NOTES AND GUIDE
BOOK FOUR

NOTE: *When explanations of words and phrases are given, these refer to the meanings within the context of each particular poem. In other contexts, they may have other meanings.*

The Explanations are given in the order in which the words and phrases occur in the poem concerned.

Explanation of Selected Terms

The following are explanations of selected terms which readers will come across in this book.

Sonnet
A sonnet is a poem of fourteen decasyllabic lines (ten syllables per line) or, rarely, octosyllabic (eight syllables per line) lines. Sonnets can be composed of an octave (eight lines) expressing one phase of an idea, and a sestet (six lines) expressing another phase of the same idea. There are several other types of sonnet form.

Ballad
A ballad is a poem or song which tells a story, usually in short stanzas (verses) and often with a refrain (a phrase repeated at intervals, usually at the end of each stanza).

Rhyme
Similar sounds in two or more words, especially at the ends of lines of poetry.

Traditional
Something (usually knowledge) which is passed from generation to generation.

PART ONE: POEMS TO SPEAK

THE WRAGGLE TAGGLE GYPSIES
After a first reading by the teacher, there can be a short discussion to decide how the students can most effectively join in the reading themselves. For a class with little previous experience of choral reading, the following arrangement is suggested:
The first two verses can be spoken by the teacher (the scene is being set and the lady is tempted). In verse three, lines 1 and 3 can be said by the teacher; line 2 can be spoken in chorus by half the class and line 4 in chorus by the other half (the lady leaves her home). The first and third lines in verse four may be taken by the teacher; line 3 by half the class in chorus and line 4 by a group of five or six students (the lord arrives to find his lady gone). Verse five may be spoken by one student (the lord determines to bring his lady back). Verse six can be said by the teacher (the lord searches for his lady) and verse seven can be spoken by one student (the lord asks the lady to explain her flight). A soloist, preferably a girl, can say the eighth verse (the lady replies to her lord) and the ninth and tenth verses may be taken by the soloists (the lord warns his lady, but she prefers the life of a gypsy and refuses to return). A discussion and questions may follow the reading.

Suggested questions
1. How did the gypsies attract the lady?
2. What did she do before she went into the street?
3. When did the lord come home?
4. What instructions did he give when he heard the lady had gone?
5. Where did the lord eventually find his lady?
6. What did the lord tell the lady she would lose if she stayed with the gypsies?
7. What did the lady finally decide to do?

sate: sat. *chamber*: room.
all her show: all her jewellery, etc.
copses: a small wood (coppice).

THERE WAS A FROG

This poem is called a ballad, i.e. a poem which tells a story. The verses of a ballad are usually short and there is an easy swinging rhythm throughout. The following is a suggested choral arrangement:

In each verse, lines 2, 5, and 6 can be said by the whole class in chorus. The teacher can read the remaining lines of verses one, two, and three; one student can speak the part of the frog in verse four, whilst another student might take the mouse's lines in verse five. In verse six, the teacher can say the first and third lines, whilst a third soloist speaks line 4. Lines 1, 3, and 4 may be taken by a soloist in the seventh verse and the first, third, and fourth lines in the eighth and ninth verses may be taken by the teacher.

THE MILTON ABBAS RHYME

This poem is suitable for a class of Secondary girls. St. Catherine is the patron saint of spinsters, and the Milton Abbey Chapel in Dorset, England, is dedicated to her. The effect of the reading will be more amusing if the poem is spoken throughout with intense seriousness. The first verse can be spoken by a group of four students. In verse two, one member of the group can speak line 1, solo; another soloist from the group can take line 2 and all four girls can say the third and fourth lines in unison. The four members of the group can take a line each of the third verse and the last line of the poem may be said by the whole class in unison.

THE TRAIN

After a preliminary reading by the teacher, the most suitable choral arrangement of this poem could be discussed by the class. One possibility would be for the whole class in chorus to speak the first three lines. One student could then read line 4; a second student could join the first to speak line 5; a third student could join the other two for line 6 and this pattern could be repeated until the twelfth line has been reached and nine students in unison have spoken it. One student could drop out of the group when the thirteenth line is said, another could drop out on line 14 (leaving seven in the group), another on line 15, another on line 16 and so on until the twentieth and last line is said by only one child. This frequently used choral pattern is called *cumulative*.

Alternatively, the arrangement could be *sequential*, i.e. after the reading of the first three lines by the whole class, student Number 1 could speak line 4, student Number 2 could say line 5, student Number 3 line 6, etc., until the twelfth line has been reached. Student Number 9 then repeats line 12 by himself, Number 8 speaks line 13, Number 7 speaks line 14, Number 6 line 15, etc., until line 20 is said by student Number 1.

pulsing: throbbing.
Cyclops: a fabled Sicilian giant with one eye in the middle of the forehead. There was supposed to be a race of Cyclops.

A DUTCH PICTURE
This poem can be spoken entirely by a soloist or by different groups of students who have some previous experience of choral reading. Group A could speak verses one and two; Group B could speak verses three and four; Group C, verses five and six and Group D, verses seven and eight. The last verse (verse nine) could then be said by the whole class in chorus.

Suggested questions
1. From where has Simon Danz just returned?
2. What did he do with the Dean of Jean?
3. Where does Simon Danz live now?
4. With what is his house furnished?
5. How is he dressed?
6. What do the tulips and the windmills represent to him?
7. What does Danz do during the winter?
8. What do the men talk about as they sit by the fire?
9. From where did the wine come? 10. What does Simon Danz think he will do at some time in the future?

singed the beard: this should not be taken literally! By piratical raids, Danz struck a blow against the King of Spain, the enemy of Holland.
hale: healthy.
Rembrandt: famous Dutch artist, 1606-1669.
Tarragon: a province in East Spain.

Poems to Enjoy, Book Four (Fifth Edition)

Don: a Spanish style of address, meaning "Mr". At one time it was a title applied only to royalty, noblemen, and similar and to indicate particular esteem for a man's role in civil society.

A LONG TIME AGO
After Group A ("light" voices) and Group B ("dark" voices) have been chosen from the class, the following would be a possible arrangement for reading aloud:
N.B. "Dark" (or "heavy") voices are heavier in quality and lower in pitch, or tone, than "light" voices.

Verse 1	
Line 1	Group B
Line 2	All the class
Line 3	Group A
Line 4	All the class
Verse 2	
Line 1	Soloist
Line 2	All the class
Line 3	Soloist
Line 4	All the class
Verse 3	
Line 1	Soloist
Line 2	All the class
Line 3	Soloist
Line 4	All the class
Verse 4	
Line 1	Group A
Line 2	All the class.
Line 3	Groups A and B
Line 4	All the class
Verse 5	
Line 1	Soloist
Line 2	All the class
Line 3	Soloist
Line 4	All the class

Verse 6	
Line 1	Group A
Line 2	All the class
Line 3	Group B
Line 4	All the class

FOREBODING

This poem by the author of 'Elephant Song' can be arranged for choral reading by individual students and groups. The class can be encouraged to discuss various likely arrangements. The *m* and *sh* consonantal sounds and the vowel sounds in lines 13, 18, and 28 need particular attention. Attention should be paid to the meaning of the various lines when the choral arrangements are being worked out. The poet seems to feel that the wild behaviour of the elements outside his beach house is, in some way, menacing.

Foreboding: a presentiment, usually of evil.
banshee: a spirit whose wailing is a portent of death.
bludgeon: to strike heavily.
dirge: a song sung at a funeral.

ELEPHANT SONG

Different combinations of solo voices and groups are possible in a reading of this poem. Experiments can be carried out with voices of different quality, e.g.

Lines 1, 2, 21, and 22	Group A (8-10 "dark" voices)	Intoned, like the ringing of a bell
Line 3	The whole class	In unison
Lines 4 and 5	Group B (6-8 "light" voices)	Line 4 slowly; line 5 intoned
Line 6	(Group B)	Sharply and stridently
Lines 7 and 8	(Group A)	With careful attention to the *sh* sounds
Lines 9 and 10	1st Soloist	Puzzled
Line 11	2nd Soloist	Angrily

Line 12	3rd Soloist	Curiously
Lines 13 and 14	4th Soloist	Line 13: Take care over "charmer's tune"!
Line 15: "The street dogs scamper":	Group B	Lightly and easily
Line 15: "The children scurry"	Group A	Urgently
Lines 16 and 17	Groups A and B	Light and "dark" voices together, maintaining their own quality
Line 18: First "Tong!"	1st Soloist	In light voice, high pitched
Line 18: Second "Tong!"	2nd Soloist	In "dark" voice, low pitched
Line 19	Group A	Intoned
Line 20	Groups A and B	Intoned

mahout: an elephant driver.
faquir: a religious devotee.

SONG OF THE FOX
In each of the verses of this seventeenth century poem, the first and third lines can be said by the teacher. Lines 2 and 8 of each verse can be taken by the whole class in unison. Line 4 of each verse ("O keep you all well there") may be said by a small selected group and lines 5-7 can be spoken by different soloists. Fox-hunting might be briefly described to the students before the reading begins.

THE HUNT IS UP
Lines 1-3 of this poem could be said by the whole class in chorus; lines 4-6 could be taken by a small group of six to eight students. Lines 1-3 of the second and third verses are suitable for a soloist and the fourth, fifth, and sixth lines of these two verses could be spoken by the small group. The reading throughout should be bright and happy.

A CARRION CROW
In each verse, lines 2 and 5 can be spoken by the whole class in unison, whilst line 4 is said by a small selected group. In verses one and three, the first and third lines may be said by the teacher, or by a student-narrator and in the second and fourth verse the first and third lines can be taken by a soloist.

THE MAKER OF CRADLES
After a first reading by the teacher there can be a discussion and some questions, for example:
1. What materials does the craftsman use to make the cradles?
2. What designs does he paint upon them?
3. Where is the gypsy babe?
4. What is his cradle?
5. Why cannot the Maker of Cradles make a lovelier cradle than the gypsy babe's?

Another reading can follow the discussion and, as the teacher speaks the main part of the poem, different soloists from the class can take the last two lines of each verse, i.e.; "Where shall I rest your little tired head? Son of my heart, lie still", she said.")

BOUND TO CALIFORNIA
Group A of five students, Group B of nine students, and Group C of fifteen students could be chosen from the class. One possible reading of this shanty could then be given as follows:

Line 1	All the class
Line 2	Group A
Line 3	Group B
Line 4	Group C
Line 5	All the class
Line 6	Group A
Line 7	Group B
Line 8	Group C

Poems to Enjoy, Book Four (Fifth Edition)

A WANDERER'S SONG

This poem can be spoken by a soloist (the teacher, or a student who has been given the opportunity to practise the lines) and two Groups, A and B. The following suggested arrangement might be attempted:

Verse 1	
Line 1	Soloist
Line 2	Group A
Line 3	Group B
Line 4	Soloist
Verse 2	
Line 1	Soloist
Line 2	Group A
Line 3	Groups A and B
Line 4	Soloist
Verse 3	
Line 1	Soloist
Line 2	Groups A and B
Line 3	Soloist
Line 4	Soloist
Verse 4	
Line 1	Soloist
Line 2	Groups A and B
Line 3	Soloist
Line 4	Soloist

yawls: small sailing-boats.
ketches: small two-masted ships.
capstan: a machine turned by bars, used for winding cable.
hooker: a small two-masted ship.
warping out: to move a vessel by hauling on the ropes attaching it to a wharf.
Moby Dick: the fictitious white whale which appears in Herman Melville's famous book, *Moby Dick*.

MERRY ARE THE BELLS
Three groups, A, B, and C may be selected from the class. In the first verse, Group A can speak Line 1; line 2 can be taken by a soloist and lines 3 and 4 can be spoken by the whole class in unison. In verse two, Group A can say Line 1, Group B, line 2 and Group C, line 3. The fourth line can be taken by the whole class. In the last verse of the poem, the first line might be said by Group A; Groups B and C can speak the second line together and the last two lines may be taken by the class in unison.

A FOX JUMPED UP
The teacher could narrate most of the poem, whilst three different soloists or groups say the lines of the Fox, the Farmer's Wife and the Farmer. When the poem has been read two or three times, the class can take turns to mime the story in groups of three, as the teacher speaks the whole poem.

PIPER PLAY
This modern poem is suitable for group and individual reading by a class experienced in choral work. After a trio of "light" voices (Group A), a quartet of "medium" voices (Group B), an octet of "dark" voices (Group C) and an octet of "light" voices (Group D) have been chosen, the following arrangement might be attempted.

Verse 1:	
Lines 1-4	Narrator
Line 5. First "Piper, play!"	Group A
Line 5. Second "Piper, play!"	Group B
Line 6	Group C
Line 7	Groups A and B, together
Line 8	Group C
Verse 2	
Lines 1-4	Narrator
Line 5. First "Piper, play!"	Group A
Line 5. Second "Piper, play!"	Group B
Line 6	Group C.
Line 7	Groups A and B, together.
Line 8	Group C.

Poems to Enjoy, Book Four (Fifth Edition)

Verse 3	
Lines 1-4	Narrator
Line 5. First "Piper, rest!"	Group A
Line 5. Second "Piper, rest!"	Group B
Line 6	Group D
Line 7	Groups A and B, together.
Line 8	Group D
Verse 4	
Lines 1-4	Narrator
Line 5. First "Night and day!"	Group A
Line 5. Second "Night and day!"	Group B
Line 6	Group C
Line 7. First "Work and play!"	Group A
Line 7. Second "Work and play!"	Group B
Line 8	Group C
Verse 5	
Lines 1-4	Narrator
Line 5. First "Piper, play!"	Group A
Line 5. Second "Piper, play!"	Group B
Line 6	Group C
Line 7. "Ripe for rest,"	Group D
Line 7. "Pipe your best,"	Group C.
Line 8	Groups C and D, together.

grimy rout: the workpeople.
warp and woof: the threads which run length wise in a loom (the warp) are crossed by other threads (the woof).
galaxies: assemblies of stars.

THE CROCODILE
The teacher can narrate this "tall story" while the whole class repeats the last two lines of each verse in unison. A discussion with questions can follow the reading.

Suggested questions
1. Where was the storyteller shipwrecked?
2. How long was the crocodile?
3. How did the storyteller trick the crocodile?

4. What did he find in the crocodile's maw?
5. How did the storyteller escape from the crocodile?

maw: stomach. *grub*: a slang word for "food". *stinted*: limited.

SIC VITA
The theme of this poem is life after death, a theme repeated in many poems of the late sixteenth and early seventeenth centuries. The twelve-line form of the poem was also popular with contemporaries of William Strode, who lived from 1600-1645. (See, for example, the following poem.)
The first line could be spoken by the whole class in chorus. Lines 2, 3, 4, 5, and 6 could be said by five different soloists; the seventh and eighth lines might be taken by the teacher, whilst lines 9-12 could be spoken by four separate groups.

Sic Vita: such is life.
Ahaz: King of Judah. (See the Bible, II Kings xvi, v. 2.)

SIC VITA
The form of this poem, by William Browne, is the same as the preceding one. The theme, however, is somewhat different. Man's life is only transitory and as impermanent as material things.
The same choral treatment can be given to it as is suggested for the previous poem.

WHEN BEGGARS RIDE
After a first reading, the class can speak the last two lines of each verse in unison, whilst the teacher reads the remainder of the poem. A discussion can follow.

Suggested questions
1. What does a wish do?
2. Where do wishes always come true?
3. What five countries does the author imply that she would like to visit?
6. What is "the Milky Way"?
5. Where are the Southern Seas?

Poems to Enjoy, Book Four (Fifth Edition)

THE FROG AND THE CROW
In the first verse, Group A ("light" voices) could speak line 1 and Group B ("dark" voices) could take line 2. The dialogue in lines 3 and 4 could be spoken by two soloists and the narrative parts could be taken by Groups A and B combined. In verse two, there could be a similar arrangement. In the third verse, a third soloist (the fish) is introduced and the narrative could again be taken by Groups A and B together. In verse four, Group A could speak line 1 and Group B, line 2. Two soloists and Groups A and B combined, speak the third and fourth lines. In the last verse, Group A could speak line 1, Group B, line 2; Groups A and B combined and a soloist, line 3, and the whole class in unison, line 4.

CASEY JONES
It is suggested that the teacher narrates most of the poem while different groups in the class speak the refrain after each verse.

hogger: engine driver.
whippoorwill: an American bird.
pink: a cabled message.

A NAUGHTY BOY
For group and individual speaking. Group A ("light" voices) could say lines 1 and 2; Group B ("dark" voices) could take lines 3 and 4 and Groups A and B, combined, might speak the fifth line. Student one could say lines 6 and 7; student two, lines 8 and 9; student three, lines 10 and 11; student four, lines 12 and 13; student six, lines 14 and 15; student seven, lines 16 and 17, and student eight, lines 19 and 20. Lines 21 and 22 could be taken by Group A; lines 24 and 25 by Group B and the twenty-third line by Groups A and B combined.

YE SPOTTED SNAKES
Verses one and three can be spoken by the teacher. The chorus (verses two and four) may be divided into parts, e.g. in both verses, lines 1, 2, 6, and 7 might be spoken by a group of "light" voices, lines 4 and 5 by a group of "dark" voices and line 3 by the whole class.

THE ONE-EYED RILEY
The refrain, throughout the reading of this poem, can be read by six different groups. The teacher can narrate verses one, four, and six, whilst each of the lines in the second, third, and fifth verses might be spoken by different individual students.

scratch: room.

BATTLE SONG
A possible choral arrangement of this early seventeenth century poem is as follows:

Line 1	First soloist
Line 2	Second soloist
Line 3	First soloist
Line 4	Group A (octet of "light" voices)
Line 5	Group B (octet of "dark" voices)
Lines 6 and 7	Groups A and B combined
Line 8	The whole class
Line 9. "They meet, they meet"	Group A
Line 9. "Now the battle comes"	Group B
Line 10	Third soloist
Line 11	Fourth soloist
Line 12	Fifth soloist
Line 13	Sixth soloist
Line 14	The whole class
Lines 15 and 16	Group B
Line 17	First soloist
Line 18	Second soloist
Lines 19-22	Groups A and B combined
Line 23	Group A
Line 24	Group B
Line 25	Group G (trio of "light" voices)
Line 26	Group A
Line 27	The whole class

Poems to Enjoy, Book Four (Fifth Edition)

Lines 28 and 29	Second soloist
Lines 30 and 31	First soloist.

succour: help.

THE SHEPHERD-BOY AND THE WOLF
This poem with a moral is suitable for narration by the teacher. The class can speak the shepherd-boy's lines in unison.

was wont: used to.
wold: open stretch of land.
forsooth: to be sure.

THE GENTLEMAN ON THE GATE
The first eight lines could be taken by the teacher, or by a student who has first read the poem. Line 9 could then be taken by student one; line 10, by students one and two; Line 11, by students one, two, and three, etc., until line 17 has been said by nine students together. The whole class may complete the reading by speaking the last two lines of the poem.

PART TWO: PICTURES IN POETRY

THE RIDE-BY-NIGHTS
After the teacher's preliminary readings, the students can be asked to draw or paint what they "see", or, alternatively, they may be encouraged to attempt the writing of their own poems on a similar theme.

crescent: the moon.
cowled: wearing hoods.
tweet: chatter.
pell-mell: confusedly.
Charlie's Wain: The Great Bear (a northern constellation or group of stars).
Milky Way: a galaxy of stars.
Sinus: the Dogstar.
Orion: a constellation. *amain*: hastily.

NIGHT SONG IN THE JUNGLE
This poem could be read aloud by two groups chosen from the class. One group could read Lines 1, 2, 5, and 6 and the other group could speak lines 3, 4, 7, and 8. The students could then be asked to illustrate the jungle scene.

FROM THE GARDENER
A poem suggesting scenes which the students should be able to illustrate after listening to the teacher's reading.

LO-YANG
For illustration by the students after two or three readings by the teacher.

THREE YOUNG RATS
This poem can be arranged for choral reading. Lines 1, 2, 3, and 4 can be spoken by four separate groups of students (three in each group). Lines 5 and 6 might be spoken by a larger group and the last two lines may be said by the whole class in chorus. After the reading, sketching and painting can begin.

flats: sandals.
demi-veils: half-veils.
sorrel: reddish-brown.

AMPHIBIAN
The students may find some difficulty with the mystical references in this poem, although the language is simple. The butterfly, whose presence is imagined by the poet ("the fancy I had today") is a representative of spiritual forces. The scene described, however, is clear enough and after the preliminary reading and a short explanation, the students can be asked to sketch and paint from the imagination.

membraned: sheet-like tissue lining the wings.
sun-suffused: the sunlight spreads over the surface of the wings as from within.
soul: the immortal, spiritual part of a human being.

Poems to Enjoy, Book Four (Fifth Edition)

IF
After two readings by the teacher, some explanation and a discussion may follow.

Verse 2
Tobacco used to be smoked in clay pipes, so that it would be impossible to smoke if the world was made of sand alone and clay was not available.

Verse 3
If all the wine-bottles were cracked and the grapes were eaten up, there would be no wine. "Sack" is a white wine which used to be imported into the United Kingdom from Spain and the Canaries.

Verse 4 A "friar" is a member of a religious order.

bald pates: bald heads. *cloisters*: convents.

Verse 5
Lines 3 and 4. There would be no music if all the fiddlers became actors.

Verse 6
If everything lasted forever, this poem could not have been completed—the poet would still be speaking or singing it.

A final reading can follow the discussion.

FROM EVENING
For illustration after one or two readings by the teacher. No explanations are required.

THE COMMON CORMORANT
A humorous poem requiring little explanation. The teacher may, however, ask the class the following questions:
1. Where does the cormorant lay its eggs?
2. Why does it choose a paper-bag?
3. What is likely to happen to the bags?
4. Why should the bears want them?

Poems to Enjoy, Book Four (Fifth Edition) 158

5. Why does the poet call the cormorants unobservant? A cormorant is a sea-bird, reputed to be extremely greedy.

THE SNAIL
The class can speak together the one or two-word fourth line of each verse, the teacher reading the remainder of the poem.

imminent: going to happen soon.
betides: happen.
chattels: possessions.
(See Notes to 'The Housekeeper'.)

SNAKE
After two or three readings and some discussion, the students can be asked to sketch and paint what they "see". A final reading will complete the lesson.

A spotted shaft: the snake.

THE SHELL
Before this poem is read, each student might be asked to bring some sea-shells to class. After they have been shown, the teacher can read through the poem twice. Each verse will need some explanation.

Verse 1
The shell is beautifully made

Verse 2
It can hardly be described in words.

Verse 3
The poet imagines the shell to be sad because the original inhabitant (the mollusc) has left it.

Verse 4
Although the shell is delicate and frail, it has, nevertheless, survived the tremendous force of the sea.

divine: God-like. Admirable as God is admirable.

forlorn: sad.
The little living will: the mollusc inside the shell.
cataract seas: stormy seas.
three-decker: large ship.
oaken spine: the keel of the ship.

THE POULTRIES
This poem can be read in conjunction with the previous poem. Little explanation should be necessary.
conundrum: a riddle.

THE WIND IN THE GRASS
For illustration after a preliminary reading.

VIGIL
After the teacher has read the poem twice, a discussion can follow. The poem tells us how a boy living near the sea watches the ships as they come in and out. Although he has no contact with them, he imagines himself to be responsible for their comings and goings.

cry them hail: welcome them. *league*: a distance of three miles.

A PIPER
This little poem can be arranged for choral reading. Lines 1 and 2 might be said by the teacher. A small group (a quartet) can speak lines 3 and 4 (as far as 'we started'). Three more students can join the group to say the words 'on every side' (line 4) and line 5. Lines 6 and 7 can be taken by two different soloists; the quartet can say lines 8 and 9 and the teacher can read the last two lines of the poem. After the reading, the students can be asked to make illustrations of the scene.

THE ISLAND
The students can be asked to speak the seventh line of the first verse ('Boom! Boom! Boom!') as the teacher reads the rest of the poem. After the reading, the students may be asked to sketch or paint any one of the pictures described, e.g. 1. The ship sailing to the island (verse one); 2. The child climbing up the cliff, 'as the stones patter

down' (verse two); 3. The child lying on top of the cliff and gazing down at the sand and the sea (verse three).

the green: the wave.
the white: the foamy crest of the wave.
grey-blue distant haze: the horizon.

THE HOUSEKEEPER
This poem can be read to the class by the teacher, together with the poem 'Snail', by John Drinkwater (PTE3 3rd Ed, p. 68) and 'The Snail', by William Cowper (PTE4 3rd Ed). A discussion with some questioning might follow the reading.

Suggested questions
1. What does the snail do when the rain comes?
2. Where does he sleep at night?
3. What happens if the snail is touched?
4. With whom does the snail eat and sleep?

After a further reading of the two poems, some comparison might be made between 'The Housekeeper' and William Cowper's 'The Snail'. The students can be shown that whereas The Snail is divided into six short verses and the first three lines of each verse rhyme (e.g. "wall", "fall", "all"; "touch", "such", "much"), 'The Housekeeper' is made up of fourteen lines and there is no separation into verses. The students might then be told, without detailed explanation at this stage, that poems containing fourteen lines, similar in form to 'The Housekeeper', are usually called sonnets.

forecast of repose: thinking of the time when he might want to rest.
domicile: house. *sanctuary*: refuge.
Quarter Day: the day on which rent should be paid.
o'nights: at night (all nights).
procure: to obtain. *chattels*: furniture.

ROMANCE
The poet describes the romantic day-dreams of the young boy. The dreams are vivid and the scenes imagined by the boy make actual

Poems to Enjoy, Book Four (Fifth Edition)

people, happenings and things seem unreal. The poem can be read to the students after some preliminary explanation by the teacher.

Chimborazo, Cotopaxi: mountain peaks in the Andes. *Popocatapetl*: a volcanic mountain (Mexico).

THE LION'S SKELETON
A discussion can follow the teacher's reading. The once-powerful lion, King of the Beasts, is reduced to a skeleton by different forces (the vultures, the elements, and the sand).

rapt: carried away.
ardors (ardours): the heat. (Latin, *ardeo*, I burn.)
sate: sat, remained.

A final reading will complete the lesson.

THE BRIDGE
This poem should be read straight through by the teacher without preliminary explanation. After the reading a discussion can follow. Verses one to four describe the bridge and the railway track, and verses five to seven describe the approach and passing of the train.

spans: reaches across from one side to the other.
cutting: an excavation for a railway track through hills or high ground.
Like arms of mute appeal: like arms raised, pleading silently.
pall: cloak of darkness (a pall is a cloth usually spread over a coffin).
red eye: red signal light.
iron thunder: the noise of the approaching train.
tawny: orange-brown in colour.
exultant: triumphant.

After a further reading the students can be asked to sketch or paint the scene described.

THE OLD STONE HOUSE
This poem which contains a vivid description of one interesting scene is very suitable for illustration work after two readings by the

teacher. No preliminary explanation should be required. The poem should be read so as to emphasise the mysterious quality of the house.

casement: a hinged window, or part of a hinged window.

I LIKE TO SEE
This poem might be read in conjunction with 'The Bridge', by J. Redwood Anderson. The poet describes the train so that it seems to have all the attributes of a horse. It "laps the miles" and "licks the valleys up". It is "supercilious" and yet "docile" and it "neighs" and "complains".

prodigious: enormous.
supercilious: contemptuously indifferent.
shanties: huts.
pare: cutting away.
Boanerges: used to mean "a loud-voiced orator".

THE CANE-BOTTOM'D CHAIR
The students can be encouraged to paint or sketch the room described by the poet, after two readings by the teacher. A small room at the top of the house ("up four pair of stairs") is the poet's favourite retreat. There, surrounded by many old, familiar things, including his favourite chair, he likes to "talk of old books, and old friends, and old times".

toast at the bars: warming at the bars of the fire.
snug little kingdom: the comfortable room at the top of the house.
nooks: corners.
knicknacks: ornaments of various kinds.
brokers: dealers in second-hand goods.
keepsakes: mementos.
rickety: unstable.
spinet: a musical instrument played with a keyboard, rather like a harpsichord.
Mameluke: Turkish slave-troop.
muffins: tea-cakes. *Latakie*: a kind of tobacco.

IN THE JUNGLE
A colourful description of the jungle scene which can be sketched or painted by the students after two or three readings by the teacher.

prick-eared: with pointed, erect ears.
ruffed: the mane stands out like a ruff. A ruff was a type of decorative, frilly collar, particularly popular in sixteenth-century Europe.
fiery meteors: like fierce, shooting stars.
spawning undergrowth: the quick-growing, fertile jungle.
sloth: laziness.
river-horse: hippopotamus.
guile: cunning.
The Jungle Spirit: the mysterious force supposed to be ever-present in the jungle.
snaring: trapping.
mazed: confused.
groves: woods.

THE MALAY KRIS
For illustration after some preliminary explanation and two readings by the teacher. A "kris" is a Malay sword and the translation describes one fine specimen.

'mid the blade was damask fateful: the blade was made of the kind of steel made in Damascus.
Kaabah: a sacred building in Mecca.
upper reaches: part of the river.

PARACHUTE
The students can be encouraged to illustrate the scene described. Little explanation should be necessary, although some discussion of the method of opening a parachute and the system used to eject a pilot from an aircraft, might interest a class of boys.

his spirit shrinks: his courage wavers.
ore: a metal-yielding mineral.

INDIA
This poem may be read in conjunction with 'In the Jungle' by Martin Armstrong (PTE4, 3rd Ed.). After two readings by the teacher and some discussion and questions, the students can be encouraged to sketch and paint the jungle scene described.

Suggested questions
1. What are the tigers said to look like?
2. What are the tigers doing in the jungle?
3. Why do you think they hunt by water-pools?
4. What are the toads doing?

CARGOES
Three different ships are described in this poem to illustrate the romance of the sea and the seafarer's life. The ships of the twentieth century carry cargoes, as did the ships of ancient times. The purpose is the same, although the goods are different.
A discussion and some questioning may follow two readings by the teacher.

Suggested questions
1. Where has the first ship come from?
2. What cargo is she carrying?
3. To what country does the second ship belong?
4. From where does the coal carried by the third ship come?

Quinquereme: a ship used for long journeys in olden times. The ship was propelled by five banks of oars pulled by slaves.
Ophir: a place in Arabia.
haven: harbour (a place where the ship would be safe).
galleon: a large sixteenth- and seventeenth-century sailing ship.
Isthmus: The Isthmus of Panama.
cinnamon: a kind of spice.
moidores: Portuguese gold coins.
pig-lead: unrefined lead, cast in blocks.
Mad March days: March is a traditionally windy, stormy month, especially near the British coastline.

After the discussion, the students can be given one verse each to illustrate.

DESERTED
This can be read in conjunction with 'The Old Stone House'. The poem can be read twice to the students. A discussion and questions to stimulate the imagination may then follow.

Suggested questions
1. How does the house lean upon the tree?
2. Of what does the noise of the wind remind the poet?
3. What does the starlight look like?
4. How many comparisons, beginning with the word "like", does the poet make?

Further work to exercise the student's imagination can take the form of suggestions and questions, e.g.
1. Stand outside the house and look at it. What do you see?
2. Stand in the porch of the house and look upwards at the sky. What can you see?
3. Move to the outside of the house. What can you hear?

After the readings and discussion and when a suitable atmosphere has been created, illustration work can begin.

lanthorn: an oil lamp.

WITH SHIPS THE SEA WAS SPRINKLED
The form of this poem (14 lines), can be compared with that of 'The Housekeeper', by Charles Lamb. The students can be told, without detailed explanation at this stage, that a poem of this kind is called a *sonnet*. Two readings by the teacher can be followed by a discussion and some questioning. After the discussion, sketching and painting of the scene can be encouraged. The illustrations can be concerned primarily with the ship the poet describes as having impressed him most.

Suggested questions
1. With what are the ships in harbour compared?

2. What are the ships doing in the harbour?
3. Where was the "goodly vessel" going?
4. How do you know that the poet liked "the goodly ship"?

veering: changing direction.
haven: safe harbour.
and lustily along the bay she strode: the ship sailed quickly and vigorously across the bay.
tackling: the ropes and pulleys attached to the sails.
apparel: clothing (but here meaning the sails of the ship).
she will brook no tarrying: she will not tolerate having to wait.

PART THREE: THE POET AS STORYTELLER

THE HANGMAN'S TREE
The teacher can narrate most of this poem, but the verses containing the replies of the father, mother, sister, and sweetheart (verses three, six, nine, and eleven) can be spoken by four different soloists from the class. After the reading, there can be a discussion and some questioning.

Suggested questions
1. Why does the person about to be hanged hope his father will pay the fee?
2. Why doesn't the father want to pay the fee?
3. What did the sweetheart come to do?
4. How did she manage to arrange for the man to go free?
5. How many people refuse to help the man?
6. Who are they?

THE SLAVE'S DREAM
This poem tells the story of a captive slave who dreams of the days of his liberty and dies before waking. A discussion and some questioning can follow the teacher's reading.

Suggested questions
1. Where is the slave?
2. Why is the rice "ungathered"?
3. What rank did the slave hold in earlier days?

4. Why did a tear fall from the dreaming man's eyes?
5. What did the slave dream he had done after kissing his children and the queen?
6. What were his bridle-reins made of?
7. How did he find his way to the sea?
8. Why did the slave smile in his sleep?
9. Why did he not feel the driver's whip?

sickle: a tool used for reaping.
Niger: a large African river.
martial clank: the warlike noise made by his sword.
tamarind: a tree, to be found in the tropics.
Caffre: Kaffir (an African).
river-horse: hippopotamus.
myriad tongues: vast number of voices.
Blast of the Desert: Desert wind.
fetter: a shackle.

A final reading can complete the lesson.

THE TOWKAY
This poem tells the simple story of the important man, who, because of many problems and "endless business", can no longer enjoy, or even notice, the beauty of flowers.
The poem should be read straight through without preliminary explanation or comment.

Towkay: an employer, commonly taken to mean an important man of business.

BALLAD
This poem should be read so that the mysterious aspect of the story is underlined. The young maiden is a kind of temptress who lures the young men of the village away to an unknown fate.
The poem can be arranged for choral speaking, the teacher acting as narrator and speaking the first three lines of verse one. A soloist, preferably a girl can take line 4. Each line in the second verse can be said by four different students; the teacher can say lines 1 and 2 of verse three and the soloist lines 3 and 4 of the same verse. The

teacher might read the rest of the poem, except for the last line which can be spoken by the whole class in unison. After the reading, a discussion can be held.

Suggested questions
1. Where was the maiden?
2. What was the boat like?
3. What did the maiden want?
4. Where did the youths go when they heard the maiden's song?
5. How many youths went with the maiden?
6. What happened to the youths?

vesper-bell: the bell rung for the evening service in Western and Greek churches.
sprite: spirit (= " person"); here, a "youth" (young man).
strand: beach.
the witching song: the song that had bewitched them.
plied the oar: began to row.
pinnace: small boat.

AN INCIDENT OF THE FRENCH CAMP
A discussion can follow the teacher's second reading or audio playing of this tale of devotion to duty.

Suggested questions
1. What city was being stormed by the French?
2. Where was Napoleon?
3. What was he thinking?
4. Where did the rider come from?
5. What news did the boy give to Napoleon?
6. What had the boy done in Ratisbon?
7. What happened to the boy after Napoleon had spoken to him?

the prone brow: bent downwards.
'twixt: from between.
vans: the wings of the bird forming part of the pattern of the war-standard, or flag.

A further reading by the teacher or playing of the audio track can complete the lesson.

THE GLOVE AND THE LIONS

The poem describes how vanity lost a lady the respect of her lover. The lady, by throwing her glove in amongst the lions, forced Count de Lorge into unnecessary danger merely to prove to herself that the Count would make sacrifices and run risks for her.

This poem is best narrated by the teacher, whilst two different students speak the lines of the King and the lady when they occur. The reading can be followed by a discussion and some questioning.

Suggested questions
1. Where were King Francis and the lords and ladies of his Court?
2. Who were the royal beasts?
3. What were the lions doing?
4. What did the lady do?
5. Why did she do it?
6. What did the Count do?
7. Where did he throw the lady's glove?
8. Why did he not return the glove to her politely?
9. What was the King's opinion of the Count's action?

sighed: loved
crowning show: the royal splendour of the scene.
ramped: the lions stood on their hind-legs with their fore-paws in the air.
main: effort.
King Francis: King Francis I of France.

THE KNIGHT'S LEAP

Two readings by the teacher can be followed by questioning and some discussion.

Suggested questions
1. Why does the knight expect the cup of wine to be his last?
2. What instructions did the knight give to his men?
3. What made it necessary for the knight to give these instructions?
4. Who is "the Altenahr hawk"?

5. What did the knight do after draining the cup of wine?
6. What alternative death was there for the knight?
7. Where was the knight found?

perforce: of necessity. *burgher*: a townsman.
mass: a Christian ceremony (the celebration of the Lord's Supper).

PAUL REVERE'S RIDE
The teacher should give a brief summary of this long poem and then read the whole of it to the students. After the reading, the poem can be divided into sections. Each section may then be read separately to the class and a short discussion with some explanation and questioning can follow the readings.

The poem relates the story of Paul Revere's ride to warn the people of Middlesex in America to be ready to defend themselves against the Regular soldiers of the British Army. The events described took place, according to tradition, during the American War of Independence. Before crossing the river to Charlestown in preparation for his ride, Revere instructed a friend to watch the movements of the British from the tower of North Church. If they marched out of the town by land, or made ready to leave by sea, the friend agreed to hang a warning light, or lights, from the tower so that Revere could observe one, or both. One light would indicate that the British were marching by land; two lights would show that they had left by sea.

Arriving at the Charlestown shore, Revere waited impatiently for the signal. When it came, two lights revealed that the British had decided to leave by sea. This was the moment Revere had waited for and as soon as the second lamp appeared in the belfry of the church, he began his ride. He rode for many miles, through the towns of Medford, Lexington and Concord and through the length and breadth of Middlesex. Because of his warnings, the inhabitants were able to defend themselves against the British soldiers and consequently disaster was averted.

Verses 1-3
Revere gives instructions to his friend and then rows over to the Charlestown shore. As he moves silently across the water, he sees the British warship, the Somerset, swinging at anchor.

Suggested questions
1. When did Revere's ride take place?
2. Where did Revere ask his friend to station himself?
3. Where was the lantern to be hung?
4. What did Revere plan to do when he saw the signal?
5. What did Revere see in the bay?
belfry: the part of a church steeple in which the bells are hung. *hulk*: the British warship.

Verses 4-6
Revere's friend wanders through the town trying to pick up information. He hears the soldiers marching through the streets to their boats and so goes to the church and climbs into the belfry-tower. As he looks out from the tower over the sleeping town and the churchyard, he is for a moment affected by the atmosphere, but recovers himself when he sees in the bay the boats carrying the British soldiers and he gives the signal, two lanterns.

Suggested questions
1. Why did Revere's friend wander through the streets of the town?
2. What could he hear in the town?
3. What did he do when he heard the grenadiers marching down to their boats?
4. What startled the pigeons?
5. What did Revere's friend do when he reached the highest window in the wall?
6. What could he see when he looked down?
7. What could he hear from the tower?
8. What distracted his attention from his dread of the belfry?

muster: the assembling of the men.
grenadiers: members of the first company of every battalion of foot-soldiers.
sombre: gloomy and dark.

Verse 7
On the Charlestown shore, Revere waits impatiently for the signal. As soon as it comes, he mounts the saddle of his horse and begins his tremendous ride.

Suggested questions
1. Why was Revere impatient and impetuous?
2. What was he doing for most of the time?
3. What did he do after seeing the first light?

saddle-girth: the belly-band of the saddle.
spectral: ghostly.

Verses 8-12
Revere begins his ride. He leaves the village and moves into the hills. He moves through the various towns of Middlesex passing his warning to all the inhabitants.

Suggested questions
1. What time did Revere arrive in Medford?
2. What did he see in Lexington?
3. What did he hear in Concord?

tranquil: peaceful.
the Mystic:
the river. *alders*: trees.

Verses 13-14
The poet notes that the battle between the Middlesex people and the British soldiers is recorded in the history books. Revere's gallant ride and the warnings he managed to give saved the inhabitants of Middlesex and his deed has gone down into history.

Suggested questions
1. Where did the farmers fight?
2. What kind of warning did Paul Revere give?
3. What did the British Regulars do?

the Red-coats: the British Regular soldiers.

Note. It is suggested that this poem be dealt with during two or three periods. A final reading by the teacher, or playing of the audio track, of the complete poem, should round off the work on it.

ANNABEL LEE
The poem tells the story of a love that is so powerful that it continues after death. The whole poem may be read through twice without explanation.

seraphs: celestial beings mentioned in both Christian and Hebrew writings.
sepulchre: tomb.

THE EMPEROR AND THE BIRD'S NEST
This poem gives us a picture of the Emperor Charles's kindness to a bird despite the uncomfortable and damp conditions which exist in his camp. The story emphasises the worth of the great campaigning Emperor who, although troubled by the responsibilities of conducting the siege, can still spare a thought for the swallow who has made herself a home upon his tent.
Two readings by the teacher or playing of the audio track can be followed by a discussion and some questioning.

Suggested questions
1. Where was the siege taking place?
2. Why were the Hidalgos impatient?
3. Where was the swallow?
4. What was the nest made of?
5. Why was the Emperor half angry and half ashamed when he heard the old Hidalgo speak?
6. What did the soldiers laugh at?
7. What happened to the swallow at the end of the siege?

swarthy: dark-complexioned.
Hidalgos: Spanish gentlemen.
dragoon: cavalryman.
Golondrina: swallow.
quaffed: drank.

Silent reading of the poem by the class may complete the lesson.

WHEN THE PLANE DIVED
This poem describes vividly the determination of the sailor to continue to take evasive action for the sake of his ship, despite being wounded and despite the relentless machine-gun attacks of the pursuing aircraft. Little explanation should be necessary and after the teacher's two preliminary readings, the poem can be left to the class to read silently.

squall: sudden, violent shower.
port the helm: to turn the ship to the left.

THE KITE
The poem gives us a picture of a man and a boy setting off to fly their kite and then watching it intently as it drifts among the clouds and the birds. The boy narrating the incident is affected by the beauty of the sky, its clouds and the flying birds.
After the teacher has read the poem twice, the class can be encouraged to sketch or paint their impression of the scene, for this poem, as well as telling a story, also presents an effective picture.

THE SAILOR'S CONSOLATION
The theme of this amusing story-poem is that, in contrast to the usual idea, it is the people on land who are to be pitied during a fierce gale and not the sailors at sea. Barney Buntline's statements are not meant to be taken with entire seriousness, for it is difficult to see how it would be possible for Billy Bowline and Barny Buntline to lie "comfortably" on deck during a hurricane and when "the sea was mountains rolling"!

A discussion can follow two readings by the teacher.

Suggested questions
1. What were the weather conditions like at sea when Barney Buntline told his friend that he pitied the people on shore?
2. Why, according to Buntline, were the people in the towns in danger?
3. Why should the townspeople envy the sailors?
4. What risks do landsmen run?
5. What weaknesses can you find in Barney Buntline's statements?

slewed his quid: moved the tobacco he was chewing from one side of his mouth to the other.
nor'wester: a wind from the north west.
quaking: shivering with fright.
spouses: wives.

A further reading by the teacher or playing of the audio track can follow the discussion.

THE BEGGAR MAID
So beautiful is the beggar maid and so sweet her character that the King determines to marry her and ignore his royal station. The teacher should read the poem twice without comment.

mien: appearance. *sware*: swore.

THE THREE FISHERS
This tragic little story tells of three fishermen who died in a storm. The theme is that work must go on despite dangerous conditions, for "men must work and women must weep".
Some questioning and a discussion can follow the teacher's reading.

Suggested questions
1. What were the fishermen thinking of as they left on their journey?
2. Why was it especially necessary for the men to work?
3. What were the fishermen's wives doing in the lighthouse tower?
4. When were the corpses found?
5. What had happened to the fishermen?

harbour bar: the shallow water at the entrance to the harbour.
night-rack: the clouds driven across the sky by the night-wind.

Silent reading of the poem may complete the lesson.

THE GOOSE
After gaining comfort and riches as a result of the stranger's gift of the goose, the old woman attempts to kill the bird. The stranger returns to take the goose away, her home is destroyed and the old woman curses the stranger.

The background of the story can be given briefly, then the teacher should read straight through the poem. The main points of the story might then be recapitulated by questioning.

Suggested questions
1. What gift did the old wife receive?
2. What happened when the old woman took hold of the goose?
3. What did the old woman do when she saw the golden egg?
4. How did the old woman's life change?
5. Why did the old woman order the goose's throat to be wrung?
6. What happened after she had given this order?
7. What did the stranger do?
8. What happened to the house after the stranger had gone?

pelf: the booty (the golden egg).
quinsy: a throat disease.

THE OLD NAVY
This is a story of a brave, but ruthless and fierce Captain of a warship, who is keen to have victory even at the cost of flogging his own men to obtain it. His character, however, is sympathetically, if briefly, described.

Four separate groups of students can speak the last two lines of one verse each, as the teacher narrates the rest of the poem. After the reading, there can be the usual discussion, with questions.

Suggested questions
1. Where was the Captain when he gave his orders to the First Lieutenant?
2. What did he tell his men?
3. Why was it necessary to capture the French ship?
4. How long did it take to defeat the French ship?
5. How did the English Captain treat the French Captain?
6. What was the English Captain's proud boast?

cannonade: a kind of ship's gun.
aft: the after (stern) end of the ship.
the gift of the gab: the gift of speech.
mounseer: monsieur (French language); sir.

A further reading by the teacher or playing of the audio track will complete the lesson.

PELTERS OF PYRAMIDS

This story tells how a group of seamen from a merchant-ship became drunk and, while ashore in Egypt, mocked at some of the sacred and dignified things they saw. Before sinking into drunken sleep, they committed an act of sacrilege by pelting one of the pyramids with stones. Whilst they were asleep the sand covered their bodies and they disappeared from sight, having paid the price for their sacrilegious behaviour.

The teacher should spend some time in introducing the story to the class, before reading it to the students or playing them the audio track. A discussion can follow the reading.

Suggested questions
1. Where was the merchant-ship?
2. Why did the men jeer at Pompey's Pillar?

THE COLUBRIAD

A "colubriad" is an epic of a snake. An epic is a long narrative poem that tells of heroic events. This poem is not, strictly speaking, an epic, for the subjects and the events are not sufficiently dignified to merit the title. It is written in mock-seriousness.

Two or three readings by the teacher or playing of the audio track should be followed by a discussion.

Suggested questions
1. Why did the kittens look horrified (aghast)?
2. What caused the poet to stop?
3. What did the poet see when he stopped?
4. What was the viper doing?
5. What did the kitten do when the viper touched its nose?
6. Where did the poet go when he saw the kitten being touched?
7. Why did he go to the hall?
8. What did the poet do when he came back with the hoe?
9. Where did he find the viper when he came back?
10. Who was with the viper?
11. What did the poet do to the snake?

Poems to Enjoy, Book Four (Fifth Edition)

aghast: horrified.
deeming: believing.
fiery hue: burning appearance.
Dutch hoe: a tool used for scraping up weeds.
if I make despatch: if I hurry.
phenomenon: (in this context) remarkable thing.
ardour: eagerness.

A further reading by the teacher or playing of the audio track should follow the discussion.

NIGHT WITH A WOLF
The man and the wolf find comfort together in face of the wildness of the elements.
Questioning and discussion can follow the teacher's reading or playing of the audio track.

Suggested questions
1. Where was the poet?
2. Where did he go for shelter?
3. What did he meet near the rock?
4. What did the wolf do?
5. What happened the next morning?

belated: coming too late.

Silent reading of the poem by the class can follow the explanations and questioning.

ELEGY ON THE DEATH OF A MAD DOG
An elegy is a poem of serious mood, often a funeral song. This poem should require little explanation, but before reading it to the class the teacher might briefly summarise the events. What is expected to happen does not happen and the good man survives the mad dog's bite.

a godly race he ran: he lived a godly life.
Islington: a district of London, England.
whelp: a puppy.

of low degree: of inferior breeding.
pique: ill-feeling.

THE REBEL SOLDIER
This poem refers to the American Civil War. The forces of the South (referred to as the rebels) were defeated by the Northern Forces. The rebel soldier is alone and far away from his home.

After the teacher's preliminary reading or playing of the audio track, four groups in the class could read a verse each.

grape-shot: shot that scatters when it is fired.
musket: an old-fashioned firearm.

A final reading by the teacher or playing of the audio track can complete the lesson.

SHAMEFUL DEATH
This story, told in the first person, gives an account of a murder and the revenge taken for it. After two readings or playings of the audio track the teacher should encourage a discussion.

Suggested questions
1. Who were the four people at the man's bedside?
2. When did the knight die?
3. How was the knight killed?
4. Why did the knight have no chance to defend himself?
5. Where was the knight caught?
6. What did the murderers, do before they hung the knight?
7. What happened to the murderers?

mass-priest: a priest whose job it is to say masses for the dead. A mass is a religious ceremony.
recreants: mean-spirited wretches.
hornbeam: a kind of tree.
pinioned: tied.

After the discussion and explanations, the teacher can give a further reading or playing of the audio track. The theme of the poem is grim revenge and pity for the dead man and his wife. This theme should be kept in mind as the reading takes place.

HORATIUS

This is an excerpt from Lord Macaulay's long poem, 'Horatius'. The treatment should be the same as for 'Paul Revere's Ride', i.e. the teacher should give a brief summary of the poem and then read the whole of it to the class. After the reading, the excerpt can be divided into sections. Each section can be read separately to the class and some questioning can follow the readings. The story is of the heroic defence of Horatius and two companions of the bridge across the river before Rome. Horatius, Spurius Lartius, and Herminius keep the attackers back whilst the bridge is being hewed down.

Verses 1-3
Lars Porsena decides to attack Rome. Together with Prince Mamilius and the traitor, Sextus, he advances towards the city.

Suggested questions
1. What oath did Lars Porsena take?
2. What happened when the citizens saw Sextus?
3. Why do you think Sextus was given this reception?

trysting day: a meeting-day.
array: army.
fast by: near to.
wrought: committed.
firmament: the sky.

Verses 4-11
The Consul fears that if the bridge is captured, Rome will be doomed. Horatius offers to defend the bridge whilst it is being hewn down and Spurius Lartius and Herminius ask to be allowed to aid him. The Consul agrees to the suggestion and the poet comments on the patriotism of the Romans of that day.

Suggested questions
1. What was the Consul afraid of?
2. What did Horatius suggest that the Consul do?

3. What did Horatius offer to do?
4. Who offered to help Horatius?
5. What does the poet say the Romans were like in the "brave days of old"?
6. What are Romans like now?

darkly: gloomily.
wax hot: engage fiercely.

Verses 12-18
The army of Lars Porsena attacks and is repulsed by Horatius and his two friends. The bridge is hewn down and, whereas Spurius Lartius and Herminius manage to reach their own shore in time, Horatius is left standing on the enemy's side of the river.

Suggested questions
1. What did the Three *ask* Sextus to do?
2. What did Sextus in fact do?
3. What happened to the bridge?
4. What did Spurius Lartius and Herminius do?
5. What happened to Horatius?

dire: dreadful.
athwart: across.
tawny: orange-brown.

Verses 19-26
Horatius is left alone, facing the enemy. He ignores Lars Porsena and Sextus and jumps into the river. Both armies wait to see his fate, but despite the fierceness of the current and despite his wounds, he manages to reach land. Lars Porsena and Sextus lament the fact that Horatius has escaped.

Suggested questions
1. What alternative dangers faced Horatius as he stood alone?
2. What action did Horatius take?
3. By whom was Horatius watched?
4. What difficulties did Horatius have to face in the water?
5. What happened to him eventually?

craven: cowardly.
surges: waves.
sore: very much.
I ween: I believe.

Verses 27-28
The poet comments that the heroic story of Horatius will be remembered often in the future.

spit: a long piece of iron or wood used for roasting meat.
shuttle: a device used in weaving.

Note. This poem can be dealt with over two or three periods. A final reading by the teacher, or by a student who reads excellently, or playing of the audio track, should complete the work on it.

A MARRIAGE RING
The wedding ring is compared with the love which prompted its giving. Although worn and tested by the cares of life, it still exists. After a brief explanation of this, the poem can be read straight through.

ABOU BEN ADHEM
Two readings of this poem by the teacher, or a student who reads excellently, or a playing of the audio track, should be followed by some questioning and a discussion.

Suggested questions
1. What did Abou see when he awoke?
2. What was the angel doing?
3. What did Abou ask the angel?
4. What did the angel reply?
5. What did Abou ask the angel to write in the book?
6. What happened on the following night?

sweet accord: peaceful harmony.

Silent reading by the class should complete the lesson.

THE CHARGE OF THE LIGHT BRIGADE

This poem, which tells the story of a gallant but futile cavalry charge, can be arranged for choral speaking. A suggested arrangement is as follows.

Verse 1	
Line 1. "Half a league".	Group A (Octet of "light" voices.)
Line 1: "Half a league".	Group B (Octet of "dark" voices.)
Line 2	Groups A and B together.
Lines 3 and 4	Groups A and B together.
Line 5	Soloist.
Line 6. "Charge for the guns!"	Soloist
Line 6. "he said:"	Groups A and B together
Lines 7 and 8	Groups A and B together
Verse 2	
Line 1	Soloist
Line 2	Group B
Lines 3 and 4	Groups A and B together
Line 5	Soloist ("light" voice)
Line 6	Soloist ("dark" voice)
Line 7	Soloist ("light" voice)
Lines 8 and 9	Groups A and B together
Verse 3	
Line 1	Soloist ("dark" voice)
Line 2	Soloist ("light" voice)
Line 3	Soloist ("dark" voice)
Line 4	Groups A and B together
Line 5	Soloist ("dark" voice)
Line 6	Soloist ("dark" voice)
Line 7	Group A
Line 8	Group B
Line 9	Groups A and B together
Verse 4	
Line 1	Soloist ("light" voice)
Line 2	Soloist ("light" voice)

Line 3	Soloist ("dark" voice)
Lines 4 and 5	Groups A and B together
Lines 6 and 7	Group A
Lines 8 and 9	Group B
Line 10	Groups A and B together
Line 11	Group B
Line 12	Groups A and B together
Verse 5	
Line 1	Soloist ("dark" voice)
Line 2	Soloist ("light" voice)
Line 3	Soloist ("dark" voice)
Line 4	Group B
Lines 5 and 6	Group A
Lines 7, 8, and 9	Group B
Lines 10 and 11	Groups A and B together
Verse 6	
Line 1	Group A
Line 2	Group B
Line 3	Group A
Lines 4, 5, and 6	The whole class in unison

The arrangement suggested above gives seventeen different soloists and two groups of eight students the opportunity to participate in the reading.

league: a distance of three miles.
sabre: a curved cavalry sword.
Cossack: Russian cavalry.

ABOUT THE EDITOR

Verner Bickley is an educationist who has led international education projects in Singapore, Burma, Indonesia, Japan, Saudi Arabia and Hong Kong. For two years, he was Chairman of Directors of the East-West Centre in Hawaii and, for ten years, was Director of the Centre's Culture Learning Institute. He has served as an adjudicator in speech and drama festivals in several countries and as President of the English-Speaking Union in Hawaii and Chairman of the English-Speaking Union in Hong Kong. He has lived and worked in Hong Kong since 1983.

Specialising in institutional linguistics, language pedagogy and international education, Dr Bickley has written extensively on language and culture and on language learning and teaching. He has served as announcer and actor in radio and TV programmes broadcast in several Asian and Pacific countries. His voice was heard regularly over the NHK in Tokyo, the Burma Broadcasting Service, Radio Republic Indonesia and Radio Malaya where he broadcast from Singapore as newsreader and as actor and narrator in radio drama, as well as in programmes for schools and colleges.

Among the dozens of scripts he has written were five in a series on the use of poetry in the language class, broadcast in BBC radio's "Listen and Teach" series. Twenty scripts written by Dr Bickley for the Japan Broadcasting Company were broadcast as the television series, "How English Works".

His books include *Reading and Interpretation* (co-authored), *Reading and Understanding* (co-authored), *A New Malayan Songbook* (co-authored), *Easy English*, *Cultural Relations in the Global Community*, *Searching for Frederick* (an autobiographical-biographical narrative), *Language and the Young Learner in Hong Kong*, and *Forward to Beijing*. The first volume of his autobiography entitled, *Footfalls Echo in the Memory*, was published in 2010 and the second volume, *Steps to Paradise and Beyond*, in 2013.

Born in Cheshire, England, Dr Bickley received two bachelor's degrees from the University of Wales, before earning an M.A. degree in education there. He was made a Licentiate of the Royal Aademy of Music (Speech and Drama) in 1955 and a Licentiate of the Guildhall School of Music and Drama in the same year. He was awarded a PhD in socio-linguistics by the University of London in 1966. He is a Fellow of the Royal Society of Arts.

Employed by the British Council for twelve years, he moved from university teaching and advisory assignments to the position of English Language Officer for Japan and First Secretary in the Cultural Department of the British Embassy in Tokyo.

Dr Bickley was founding Director of the Hong Kong Government's Institute of Language in Education (which was incorporated into the Hong Kong Institute of Education after his retirement) and an Assistant Director of Education.

Dr Bickley was made a Member of the Order of the British Empire in 1964.

ABOUT THE EDITOR

Verner Bickley is an educationist who has led international education projects in Singapore, Burma, Indonesia, Japan, Saudi Arabia and Hong Kong. For two years, he was Chairman of Directors of the East-West Centre in Hawaii and, for ten years, was Director of the Centre's Culture Learning Institute. He has served as an adjudicator in speech and drama festivals in several countries and as President of the English-Speaking Union in Hawaii and Chairman of the English-Speaking Union in Hong Kong. He has lived and worked in Hong Kong since 1983.

Specialising in institutional linguistics, language pedagogy and international education, Dr Bickley has written extensively on language and culture and on language learning and teaching. He has served as announcer and actor in radio and TV programmes broadcast in several Asian and Pacific countries. His voice was heard regularly over the NHK in Tokyo, the Burma Broadcasting Service, Radio Republic Indonesia and Radio Malaya where he broadcast from Singapore as newsreader and as actor and narrator in radio drama, as well as in programmes for schools and colleges.

Among the dozens of scripts he has written were five in a series on the use of poetry in the language class, broadcast in BBC radio's "Listen and Teach" series. Twenty scripts written by Dr Bickley for the Japan Broadcasting Company were broadcast as the television series, "How English Works".

His books include *Reading and Interpretation* (co-authored), *Reading and Understanding* (co-authored), *A New Malayan Songbook* (co-authored), *Easy English*, *Cultural Relations in the Global Community*, *Searching for Frederick* (an autobiographical-biographical narrative), *Language and the Young Learner in Hong Kong,* and *Forward to Beijing*. The first volume of his autobiography entitled, *Footfalls Echo in the Memory*, was published in 2010 and the second volume, *Steps to Paradise and Beyond: Hawaii to China, Saudi Arabia, Hong Kong and Elsewhere*, in 2013.

Born in Cheshire, England, Dr Bickley received two bachelor's degrees from the University of Wales, before earning an M.A. degree in education there. He was made a Licentiate of the Royal

Aademy of Music (Speech and Drama) in 1955 and a Licentiate of the Guildhall School of Music and Drama in the same year. He was awarded a PhD in socio-linguistics by the University of London in 1966. He is a Fellow of the Royal Society of Arts.

Employed by the British Council for twelve years, he moved from university teaching and advisory assignments to the position of English Language Officer for Japan and First Secretary in the Cultural Department of the British Embassy in Tokyo.

Dr Bickley was founding Director of the Hong Kong Government's Institute of Language in Education (which was incorporated into the Hong Kong Institute of Education after his retirement) and an Assistant Director of Education.

Dr Bickley was made a Member of the Order of the British Empire in 1964.

ABOUT PROVERSE HONG KONG

Proverse Hong Kong, co-founded by Gillian and Verner Bickley, is based in Hong Kong, with growing regional and international connections.

Verner Bickley has headed cultural and educational centres, departments, institutions and projects in many parts of the world. Gillian Bickley has recently concluded a career as a university teacher of English Literature, spanning four continents. Proverse Hong Kong draws on their combined academic, administrative and teaching experience as well as varied long-term participation in reading, research, writing, editing, reviewing, publishing and authorship.

Proverse Hong Kong has published novels, novellas, single author short story collections, non-fiction (including memoirs, biography, war and travel diaries and journals, fictionalised autobiography, history, sport), single-author poetry collections, editions of nineteenth-century writing, academic and young teen books. Other interests include academic works in the humanities, social sciences, cultural studies, linguistics and education. Some Proverse books have accompanying audio texts. Proverse editors work with texts by non-native-speaker writers of English as well as by native English-speaking writers.

Proverse welcomes authors who have a story to tell, wisdom, perceptions or information to convey, a person they want to memorialise, a neglect they want to remedy, a record they want to correct, a strong interest which they want to share, skills they want to teach, and who consciously seek to make a contribution to society in an informative, interesting and well-written way.

The name, *Proverse*, combines the words "prose" and "verse" and is pronounced accordingly.

SOME EDUCATIONAL BOOKS FROM PROVERSE

Jockey, by Gillian Bickley (when Gillian Workman). Hong Kong, 1979. Pbk. 64pp.
ISBN-10: 962-85570-3-3; ISBN-13: 978-962-85570-3-5.

Poems to Enjoy: Book 1, Edited by Verner Bickley. HK & UK: 2012. Pbk. 136 pp. (inc. 35 b/w original line-drawings & Teacher's and Student's Notes). With audio CDs. ISBN 978-988-8167-54-8.

Poems to Enjoy: Book 2, Edited by Verner Bickley. HK & UK: 2013. Pbk. 136pp. (inc. 37 b/w original line-drawings & Teacher's and Student's Notes). With audio CDs. ISBN 978-988-8167-51-7.

Poems to Enjoy: Book 3, Edited by Verner Bickley. HK & UK: 2013. Pbk. 166 pp. (inc. 39 b/w original line-drawings & Teacher's and Student's Notes). w. audio CDs. ISBN 978-988-19934-1-0.

Poems to Enjoy: Book 4, Edited by Verner Bickley. HK & UK: scheduled, 2014. Pbk. *c.*174 pp. (inc. *c.*41 b/w original line-drawings & Teacher's and Student's Notes).
With audio CDs. ISBN 978-988-8167-50-0.

Poems to Enjoy: Book 5, Edited by Verner Bickley. HK & UK: scheduled, 2015. Pbk. *c.*200 pp. (inc. *c.*36 b/w original line-drawings & Teacher's and Student's Notes).
With audio CD(s) / DVD(s). ISBN 978-988-8167-49-4.

Spanking Goals and Toe Pokes: Football Sayings Explained, by T. J. Martin. HK & UK, 2008. ISBN-13: 978-988-99668-2-9.

Teachers' and Students' Guide to the Book and Audio Book, 'The Golden Needle: the Biography of Frederick Stewart (1836-1889)'. Proverse Hong Kong Study Guides. E-book. ISBN-10: 962-85570-9-2; ISBN-13: 978-962-85570-9-7. 24Reader e-book edition (2010), ISBN-13: 978-988-19320-5-1.

THE PROVERSE INTERNATIONAL LITERARY PRIZES

THE INTERNATIONAL PROVERSE PRIZE

The Proverse Prize, an annual international competition for an unpublished single-author book-length work of fiction, non-fiction, or poetry, the original work of the entrant, submitted in English (translations are welcome) was established in January 2008. It is open to all who are at least eighteen on the date they sign the entry form and without restriction of nationality, residence or citizenship.

The objectives of the prize are: to encourage excellence and / or excellence and usefulness in publishable written work in the English Language, which can, in varying degrees, "delight and instruct". Entries are invited from anywhere in the world.

Entry forms available each year from	No later than 14 April
Closing date for entry forms, fees and entered work	30 June
Judging	July-September
Semi-finalists announced	No later than November

THE INTERNATIONAL PROVERSE POETRY PRIZE (SINGLE POEMS)

Entry forms, entry fees, and entered work received from	7 May
Closing date for entry forms, fees and entered work	30 June
Judging	July-September
Winners announced	No later than November

More information, updated from time to time, is available on the Proverse Hong Kong website: proversepublishing.com

FIND OUT MORE ABOUT PROVERSE AUTHORS BOOKS AND EVENTS

Visit our website:
http://www.proversepublishing.com
Visit our distributor's website: www.chineseupress.com

Follow us on Twitter
Follow news and conversation: <twitter.com/Proversebooks>
OR
Copy and paste the following to your browser window and follow the instructions:
https://twitter.com/#!/ProverseBooks

"Like" us on www.facebook.com/ProversePress
Request our free E-Newsletter
Send your request to info@proversepublishing.com.

Availability

Most books are available in Hong Kong and world-wide from our Hong Kong based Distributor,
The Chinese University Press of Hong Kong,
The Chinese University of Hong Kong, Shatin, NT,
Hong Kong SAR, China.
Email: cup-bus@cuhk.edu.hk
Website: www.chineseupress.com

All titles are available from Proverse Hong Kong
http://www.proversepublishing.com
and the Proverse Hong Kong UK-based Distributor.

We have stock-holding retailers in Hong Kong,
Canada (Elizabeth Campbell Books),
Andorra (Llibreria La Puça, La Llibreria).
Orders can be made from bookshops
in the UK and elsewhere.

Ebooks
Most of our titles are available also as Ebooks

www.ingramcontent.com/pod-product-compliance
Lightning Source LLC
Chambersburg PA
CBHW071116160426
43196CB00013B/2585